PLAN

WHILE YOU STILL

CAN

16
END-OF-LIFE CHECKLISTS
YOU NEED NOW

WHAT OTHERS ARE SAYING ABOUT
PLAN WHILE YOU STILL CAN

"Your book would have been a blessing to have had when my father died in 2002. Looking back there were so many items that should have been taken care of differently than they were, hindsight is indeed 20/20 – I will recommend your book to my friends and family."

Cynthia Stubbs
Property Manager

"After being in the ministry for more than twenty years, what I learned in this book could have helped many of the hundreds I have walked thru end-of-life journeys with, more than anything I gave them. A huge thank you!"

Randy Carroll
Southern Baptist Minister

"This book is the ultimate resource for anyone facing the future passing of a loved one. Mr. Burrows not only shows you what you need to do but does so in a way that easy to understand and simple to implement. If you have an aging parent, then this book is a must read – full of strategies to help you remove much of the stress involved with end-of-life planning."

Patrick Snow
Author of *Creating Your Own Destiny*

"An extremely good 'check list' for us who may be left to handle the difficult end-of-life tasks for family."

Virginia "Taye" Cook
Prayers n' Paws Doberman Rescue

"As a person who is living with the last and most advanced stage of breast cancer, I have thought about what dying might be like, and how the process of dying and death will impact my husband and four children.

I envision Don's book as one that would not only help them, but me! As the organizer in our family, I can see myself helping them in the process, should I receive a terminal prognosis.

Everyone should read this book as a means to dispel myths, eliminate guesswork, and minimize anxiety associated with, 'how do we handle this?'

Don, after reading your book, I felt emotional, empowered, and so inexplicably at peace."

Wendi Fox Pedicone
Writer, Motivational Speaker, and Author of
Hanging Out With Lab Coats: Hope, Humor & Help
for Cancer Patients and Their Caregivers

"Don, I finally had the courage to read the book just now and it really hit home to what my family is facing in light of my Father's illness. You've done an excellent job at sharing your experiences as well as putting an outline together for the reader in helping them through the process.

People need to read this book before they need to use it. Believe me – when my Dad was first diagnosed – I just couldn't bring myself to read the draft you sent me – my mind was numb and on overload all at the same time. I'm glad that many of the issues you addressed, my parents had made sure to take care of long before illness became a part of their life, but you brought up other issues that we are only now beginning to deal with and I hope to use this as a guide."

Dawn Julen

"I suspect that for those who have firsthand experience with the ultimate transition of a parent, the book will be a jarring reminder of the opportunities lost, the errors made and the deeds undone that often come with the crystal clear vision of hindsight . . . particularly when that vision is enhanced by the lens this splendid work provides. In my case the view was somewhat blurred by some long suppressed tears.

Plan While You Still Can is a celebration of life, or more importantly, living. Birth and death are the bookends; this is about treasuring and valuing the story in between. It offers a way of preparing for the inevitable event that still somehow takes us by surprise. Even when a loved one's diagnosis is 'terminal', we are somehow surprised by the sense of panic, or whirling emotions, or flood of familial flotsam that so often accompanies an experience that, none-the-less, unifies us all."

JonScott Williams
Organization Development Consultant

"I was overwhelmed by the information packed into each section. I read the copy I had in a couple of days as I couldn't seem to put it down, I then dropped it off to my sister to read and this started the dialogue between us of 'oh my gosh, we really need to get started.'

As a result we have started that process, and my parents have moved closer to finalizing their plans and organizing their affairs. Thanks so much for the time you took to write such a powerfully practical and timely book. Had it not been for this book we most likely would have found ourselves planning everything after it was too late. Thanks again."

Craig Hardy
President, Covenant Homes

"Donald's book, *Plan While You Still Can*, is a great way to begin the conversations we all need to have with our families. The check list format is a non-threatening way to have these discussions. Every family can use this guide."

Sally J. Brown, retired, and
Larry Brown, Superior Court Bailiff

"*Plan While You Still Can* is clearly written from the heart of someone who has experienced the challenges that go along with aging parents and aging in society. In my line of business I see far too often a lack of planning when it comes to our last wishes and the wishes of our parents. This is a must read for individuals that want an easy sixteen step process that will help eliminate future frustration and family turmoil."

Terry Wiles
Wiles Wealth Management

"Inevitably we are all faced with the loss of a family member or the deteriorating health of parents, spouse or children. This book gives such a clear, no-nonsense approach in dealing with difficult decisions. This is a MUST HAVE book for anyone, so when we are faced with these difficult decisions, we have a way of navigating through the options in a logical and clear, instead of an emotional and chaotic method. The personal examples were extremely helpful in demonstrating how each item on the checklist came into play. Thank you, Don, for sharing so much of yourself to help others."

Darlene Geyer
Retired Loan Consultant/Banker

"Donald's lists are so practical and straight forward. When my Meme entered hospice care, four generations of our family used these lists to focus our efforts in meaningful ways to her benefit. Our intentions were always well meaning but without these lists, much valuable time would have been wasted. Our gratitude to Donald for producing such insightful tools and sparing us some heartache."

Angie Scharbau
Non-Profit Executive Director/CEO/Daughter

"When looking through your book, Don, I thought of the thousands of people that will be helped by reading such a power packed book of information before a person has to face a death alone.

As a licensed Funeral Director in the State of Washington, I have seen what families go through when they are totally unprepared for the worst time in their lives. It is often hard, and certainly painful, to sort out these mixed feelings. And at times, you will not want to deal with the problems at all. Such feelings are normal, though filled with pain. There are always hard decisions that have to be made; you have made it easy for a family to sit down and review the inevitable before a death occurs. *Plan While You Still Can* is a great book Don! Keep up the good work."

Neily W. Bissette
Vice President Marketing
Sunset Hills Memorial Park and Funeral Home

PLAN
WHILE YOU STILL
CAN

16
END-OF-LIFE CHECKLISTS
YOU NEED NOW

DONALD M. BURROWS

AVIVA
PUBLISHING

Donald M. Burrows
C/O Acorn Consulting Inc.
PO Box 1800
Marysville, WA 98270
Telephone: 800.597.9972
Orders@PlanWhileYouStillCan.com; or *www.PlanWhileYouStillCan.com*

ISBN: 978-1-890427-90-0

Library of Congress Control Number: 2006934910

Editor: Karen Druliner
Production Coordinator: Patrick Snow, *www.CreateYourOwnDestiny.com*
Cover Design: Kathi Dunn, *www.Dunn-Design.com*
Typesetting: Ad Graphics, Inc., *www.TheBookProducer.com*
Printing: Central Plains Book Mfg., *www.CentralPlainsBook.com*
Publisher: Aviva Publications, Lake Placid, NY *www.avivapubs.com*
Web site: Tone Dog Studios, *www.tonedog247.com*
Proofreader: Cindy Johnson, *Cindy@CindyJohnson.info*

Printed in the United States of America

First Edition

2 4 6 8

For additional copies of this book, please see the Quick Order Form at the back.

DEDICATION

For Mac and Nancy, Konrad and Marguerite, and Grace.
Glad I could help.

And for Eunice, for whom I think I was too late.
Rest in Peace.

MY THANKS

This book has been a while in the making. I would like to thank the people whose help has made this book a reality.

My thanks to my wife, Karin, for patiently rereading, pen in hand.

My thanks to Eddie A. for taking the time to feel and reflect upon the meaning behind each and every word.

My thanks to Karen D. for giving of her time to provide three rounds of editing and topic ideas along the way.

My thanks to John and Tandy G., Tom J., Diane and Larry K., Dr. Sheila M., Deb F., Esq., the Rev. David Poland, Rudy O., Esq., and May T. for your reactions, suggestions and input.

My thanks to my support team from Klemmer Session 78, and particularly to my buddy, Randy C.

My thanks to my production coordinator, Patrick Snow, for his enthusiasm and counsel.

My thanks to my daughter, Jen H., for her feedback; she has always wanted to be thanked in a book.

My thanks to Tim H., Esq., Jen's husband, for proofreading the final product, with his attorney's eye for detail.

My thanks to JonScott W. for making me the beneficiary of his compassion and his intellect.

And finally, my thanks to my sister-in-law, Lynne J. This book came about because of a conversation Lynne and I had shortly after she received the call that her mother, Grace G., was diagnosed with an inoperable cancer.

Thank you Lynne, for rapping me on the forehead and saying a loud *"HELL-O?"* when at first I failed to grasp that you were serious when you said my experience and ability in helping others make end-of-life planning decisions are valuable and should be shared with others.

SYNCHRONICITY

On July 18, 2004, three things occurred within 12 hours of each other:

- Grace G. died.
- John G., Grace's husband and Lynne's stepfather, died.
- I completed the first draft of *Plan While You Still Can.*

As two doors closed, a new one opened. I find the synchronicity of the three events quite astonishing.

In 2004, on her birthday, my wife, Karin, discovered a lump in her breast, and our lives took a sudden turn while a lot of things went on hold. After two rounds of chemotherapy, one round of radiation, a double mastectomy, an oophorectomy, a complete household move from North Carolina to Washington state and another surgery once we got here, Karin is back on the road to good health and I am re-engaging with this book.

PREFACE

When Don Burrows first told me about his plans for this book, my first thought was, Gee...why didn't *I* think of that? And then my second thought was, Gee...why *didn't* I think of that?

Many people of faith, while devoted and devotional in their daily lives, are still reliant upon their spiritual leaders for helping them through the nitty-gritty *details* that accompany a loved one's death (or the preparation for one's own), as well as the grief process itself. It is a part of our calling, as clergy, to assist people with these details, but it can also be quite time-consuming and even redundant.

Don has provided us professional care-givers with this book, a means of helping many people prepare *in advance* for addressing those myriad details. And, while it will be a helpful addition to the library of any house of worship, even those who do not consider themselves particularly religious will find it a useful guide for preparing for end-of-life issues.

Having recently commended my own father to God's eternal care – and having had access to Don's *manuscript* for a year or so prior to that event – I can *personally* testify to the author's insights and organizational skills. Thank you, Don, for *ministering to me*, even though you didn't know that you were doing so. I look forward to being able to recommend this book to many others for years to come.

Gratefully,
Pastor Dave Poland
Gwynedd Square Presbyterian Church
Lansdale, Pennsylvania
December, 2006

TABLE OF CONTENTS

---

* From Jimmy Buffett's song, "Breathe In. Breathe Out. Move On."

OUR GERIATRIC PLATE
IS OVERFLOWING

What makes me think I have earned the right to offer suggestions and guidance on how to react when you get the call that your mother or your father, a relative, loved one, partner or dear friend has been diagnosed as "*terminal*?"

I am not a social worker, an attorney, or a psychologist.

However, over the last 14 years, I have gained a significant measure of knowledge and first-hand experience helping people organize themselves and their families to react and respond effectively when they get the call advising them that a parent has been diagnosed with a terminal condition.

My father, Malcolm, died of cancer in 1992; my father-in-law, Konrad, died of cancer in 1995; my mother-in-law, Marguerite, died of pneumonia in 1996, and my mother, Nancy, died of a stroke in 2002. In May 2003, my sister-in-law, Lynne, learned that her mother, Grace, had just been diagnosed with an inoperable cancer. I was deeply involved in all of their transitions from living to dying to death, and with each, gained more knowledge about what issues and needs could be anticipated so that the inevitable could happen more smoothly, with less anguish and confusion and with less strain on all involved.

When I went to Seattle to assist Lynne, I spent five days helping her make a series of arrangements for Grace's care. In that time, between the two us, we:

- Arranged to have Grace's trust rewritten
- Made all medical arrangements for Grace's follow-up care as well as that of Lynne's stepfather, John
- Revised and adjusted all banking and investment relationships to address Grace's new situation
- Made arrangements for Grace's interim living care
- Made permanent arrangements in a retirement home that offered graduated care as Grace's needs evolved, and
- Took the first steps to begin sorting 40 years of accumulated personal possessions in preparation for selling Grace and John's home.

Following an experience-based plan smoothed out the process and considerably reduced the stress for both of us.

On the evening of our third day, when Lynne and I were reviewing all we had accomplished and what still needed our attention, she told me that I had a gift for this sort of thing and urged me to create a pamphlet or set of guidelines or a checklist—something to help others when they are suddenly faced with the "terminal" call from their parent or their physician. That was the genesis of *Plan While You Still Can.*

The book's subtitle is: *16 End-of-Life Checklists You Need Now.* *"Now"* is the key word. This book is intended for those who wish to *anticipate* the need for end-of-life planning, rather than reacting to it later, with a regretful knee-jerk reaction.

Everyone who knew I was writing this book was encouraging. Many recounted stories of spouses, parents, siblings, children, family members and friends who procrastinated, putting off thinking about and planning for the realities of old age until the unexpected illness or death of a loved one forced the survivors to make hasty and poorly-thought-out decisions that often proved unnecessarily painful, disruptive and costly.

According to the American Association of Retired Persons *(www.AARP.org)* and the National Alliance for Caregiving (a nonprofit in Bethesda, MD – *www.caregiving.org*) more than 44 million Americans are engaged in caring for elderly relatives or friends. The Department of Labor estimates that by 2008, 54 percent of the workforce will be providing some sort of care for an elderly person.

In 1999, the MetLife Mature Market Institute *(www.MetLife.com/maturemarket.html)* estimated that 16 percent of employees quit their jobs and 13 percent retired early because they were unable to manage their full-time jobs successfully and still provide care-giving help to someone else. (*AARP Bulletin,* May 2006, p. 18.) As a nation, we have a lot on our geriatric plate. It is clear we are approaching critical mass and we need to take action.

This book will be helpful to:

Seniors

- Who may be alone or for whom time may be a growing concern
- Who want to involve and help their children deal with forthcoming life changes
- Whose situation is not critical but who wish to start thinking about their needs

Families

- With forward-looking parents or relatives who wish to plan before the need is thrust upon them

Siblings

- Who want to work together to make rational end-of-life plans with their parents or with each other in hopes of avoiding conflict among themselves later on

Baby-Boomers; Children of Elderly Parents

- Who are healthy and trying to stay ahead of the curve
- Who together are evaluating and comparing long-term care facilities

Caregiver Organizations and Support Groups

- In religious or community-support groups for the elderly, all of whom may be facing similar problems
- In religious or community support groups for children of aging parents
- In nursing homes, hospice organizations, and hospitals
- In social services agencies
- In grief counseling

<u>Professionals providing a wide range of legal, medical, and other forms of advice and counsel</u>

- To the elderly, their children, and other caregivers

<u>Corporations</u>

- Desiring to maintain productivity and help their employees

<u>You</u>

- To help you remain calm, centered, organized, strong and in control when you learn that someone you love is "terminal."

One of my friends told me that when I used the word "you" throughout the book, she never took it to mean you-singular, as I intended. Rather, it felt to her like I was referring to her, her parent and all six sibs. After all she had been through she said, the emotional results of her interpretation were draining.

This book is based on my unique experiences. I have intended it to be a source of mind-jogging questions to help you and your loved ones anticipate, think about and talk about topics that may not necessarily be on your radar screen until you picked up this book.

Because I know that my experiences have been and will continue to be different from yours, I want to stress that you and your loved ones should use this book as a framework for thought, not as the basis for making your own final decisions.

AND FINALLY

Because I want this be a highly portable, easy-to-carry and easy-to-use reference, I have structured each chapter as a checklist of **yes** / **no** questions.

At the beginning of each chapter, you will find a section titled **My comments to you** followed by material *in italics*. In some cases, you will also find italicized material within a chapter. As you read the *italics*, I am speaking to you and sharing with you my own experiences.

At the end of each chapter, you will find the section **NOTES: SUMMARY OF "NO" POINTS.** I suggest using that space to summarize the **"NO"** items you have identified in that chapter, items that will require follow-up. It might be helpful for you and your parent or loved one to answer the questions separately, and then compare answers. Often people are more honest in their writing when the pressure is off than when they are face-to-face.

After you have completed all of the chapters, I encourage you to cross-reference, transfer, and summarize the entire **NO** points into the **NOTES: SUMMARY OF ALL "NO" POINTS** in Appendix A at the end of the book.

While writing this book has been a cathartic experience for me, I want to stress that I am not a trained professional in any of the sixteen areas I will discuss. There is absolutely no substitute for competent professional guidance as you help your loved ones make plans and arrangements.

Please remember: I am sharing my experiences only in order to provide you with ideas and perspectives from my own experiences; I am not suggesting you, your parent, or other members of your family base decisions and actions on my particular situations.

Having made one disclaimer, let me offer another. As an only child, I had no siblings with whom to contend, consult, lean on, negotiate, satisfy or take into account as I made arrangements with, and for, my parents. As you consider the questions in each chapter, please keep in mind the needs, requirements and expectations of other family members and friends. This will be a fragile time for everyone. Tempers can be short and emotions can be high for everyone. Breathing deeply and sharing frequent hugs help.

A note on the words "parent," "parents," "loved one" and "loved ones." As you read you may notice that sometimes I use the words "parent" or "parents," and sometimes I use "loved one" or "loved ones." Practically speaking, the questions are relevant to anyone you love. If it helps you to personalize the situation and feel a greater sense of immediacy and urgency to answer and resolve the questions, please replace "parent" or "loved one" with an actual name.

RESOURCES

Appendix B contains a list of resources you may find helpful. In addition, I frequently update my website *www.PlanWhileYouStillCan.com* (also reachable through *www.Donald-Burrows.com*) with new information, so please bookmark the site and stop in from time to time. I invite you to share any experiences you wish to, or to make suggestions for new chapters to be included in future editions of *Plan While You Still Can*. If you have questions, please click on "I Have a Question" and I will do my best to respond as quickly as possible.

I hope you will find this a beneficial resource that helps you and your loved ones face life's ultimate situation calmly and courageously.

Donald M. Burrows
Marysville, WA
July, 2007

PART I

AROUND
THE EDGES

1

And How Are You Holding Up?

*M**y comments to you:** Please – no matter where you are in the process of caring for your parent or loved one, make time, and take time, for yourself. If you get nothing more out of this book than positive forward momentum from implementing the contents of this chapter, both you and your loved one will be better off than if you had not.*

*If you are the child of an elderly parent or loved one, please know that I have been where you are now, five times. I have learned that during this time you and your loved one both need to have **emotional support systems** available. Sometimes the emotional support system can be as small as a single individual willing to simply listen to you. On other occasions, it may be a book group, people with whom you share a religious affiliation, a competent counselor, a best friend, your buddies at the coffee shop, a group of soccer moms, the local hospice or United Way, or any of the many service agencies listed in the government section of the white pages of the telephone book under Health and Human Services or on the Web at www.hrsa.gov*

for the Department of Health and Human Services – Health Resources and Services Administration.

My mother's name was Nancy. Her group consisted of four close friends at her retirement home and a couple she met through my wife, Karin, and me. My group consisted of Karin, my children, (Jen and Chris), my friends at the local coffee shop, and two good friends.

When I Googled **emotional support systems**, I was directed to a number of sites, among them, Lance Armstrong's LiveStrong site (www.livestrong.org) where I found a wealth of practical information.

Emotional support is available, so even if you have a big red **S** like Superman on your chest, you need not, and should not, undertake this journey alone. Hands extended in support, caring and friendship abound. Some of them may be obvious, and for others you may need to search.

For the last four years of her life, Mom lived 10 minutes away from Karin and me. As I look back on that time, I recall complaining a lot, venting a lot, and receiving solace, advice and comfort from Karin and others who had either been down the same road, or were on it as well.

At times I felt like I was being a bad son when I complained about Mom's demands on my time, her interrupting phone calls or drop-in visits in the middle of my work day "just to say hi." (*I am self-employed and work at home, and thus was "fair game.") I complained about the many frustratingly repetitious conversations we had to go over things we had already discussed and agreed upon. Karin's words, voiced more than once, were these: "You are not a bad son; you are just human."*

At one point in his career, Dad was a banker; he counseled many new widows and widowers. He encouraged them to give themselves at least a year before making and acting upon any significant decisions because in his experience, it took at least that long for head and heart to return to something approximating normal.

Hearing his voice now, four years after Mom's death, I acknowledge I did not follow his advice. Rather, I got back to work, fast, and made some important decisions, fast. In retrospect, I wish I had heeded Dad's advice and given myself time to just "be."

QUESTIONS: And How Are You Holding Up? (Yes or No)

___ 1. Do you have your own emotional support system in place?

___ 1a. Who makes up your support system and what do you need from each person? _____

_____

_____

_____

_____

_____

_____

_____

_____

____ 1b. Have you shared your thoughts, needs, fears and hopes with each of these people, so that they clearly understand your feelings?

____ 1c. Is there anyone who is unable to provide the emotional support you need?

____ 1d. If so, have you decided how you want to proceed?

____ 2. Have you thought about the impact that "all of this" is having and will have on your:

____ 2a. emotions?

____ 2b. time – for yourself, your family and your surviving parent?

____ 2c. family life?

____ 2d. sex life?

____ 2e. relaxation and time to recharge your batteries?

____ 2f. priorities?

____ 2g. finances?

____ 2h. your job?

_____ 2i.   your friends?

_____ 2j.   your pets?

_____ 2k.   your goals?

_____ 2l.   your future?

_____ 2m. your life?

_____ 3.   Have you considered how you will cope with "all of this" and specifically how you will rejuvenate yourself?

_____ 4.   If you have siblings, have you talked all of this over with them?

_____ 5.   Have you and your siblings been able to come to an agreement about dividing up the care-giving responsibilities – schedules, activities, making trade-offs – all the things you probably learned to do when you and your siblings were growing up? *This could also include working out daily living arrangements, like possibly sharing grocery shopping, cooking and cleaning responsibilities; providing transportation to/from the doctor; arranging family visits and holiday/vacation schedules; coming to agreement on how expenses are to be shared.*

While it may seem obvious, I think it bears saying that when there is more than one child involved in the care-giving process, the potential for tension, *brittle egos, and bruised feelings increases. (**Please see Chapter 2 – <u>Siblings and Relatives</u>**)*

So, while I know that the preceding points have to do with emotional issues, this seems to me an appropriate place to offer a non-emotional, tangible suggestion: Whether you have siblings or not, I urge you to dedicate space in your planner, or get a diary or a notebook and organize it by category of activity. Write down and save everything, and I mean everything, you experience throughout this entire process:

- *Names*
- *Titles*
- *Organizations*
- *Addresses*
- *Phone/fax/private line numbers*
- *Websites/e-mail addresses*
- *Detailed dated notes of who said what and who will do what by when*
- *A "Waiting For" section to track things people have committed to send to you*
- *Business cards of each person with whom you have dealings*
- *Anything else I missed that you remembered*

When Karin's father, Konrad, was dying and our sister-in-law, Lynne, was helping Karin and me, she organized a little notebook containing data by cate-

gory. Later on, she brought it with her when she came to Seattle after she got the call that her Mom, Grace, had an inoperable cancer. It was so handy. We found ourselves seeking help from several of the same people who had helped us with Konrad, and it provided us with an effective blueprint to follow.

Managing all of this information while providing care is tedious and emotionally draining. However, having gone through it five times, I can state with certainty that organizing all the information and keeping it current expedited the process and reduced stress for all concerned.

NOTES: SUMMARY OF "NO" POINTS:

*As you complete this and subsequent chapters, my assumption is that you will respond **"NO"** to some questions.*

*The section entitled '**NOTES: Summary of "NO" Points**' appears at the end of each chapter in the hope that it will increase the book's utility by providing you with a place to record the items you and your parent have decided will require additional attention.*

As you proceed through the chapters, if you note recurring themes, they may indicate several related need areas that merit everyone's attention.

You will also find cross-referenced summary pages in Appendix A.

Chapter 1:
And How Are You Holding Up?
NOTES: SUMMARY OF "NO" POINTS

2

Removing the Hassle from Your Loved One's Life

My comments to you: Mom had one major stroke and a number of smaller ones (called Transient Ischemic Attacks, or TIAs for short) before her final one in July 2002. As a result of her first stroke, her memory and her vision would come and go. Mostly go.

Once she recuperated, she was not in physical pain, but she was definitely annoyed. I am a guy, so naturally I tried to "fix" things. I found myself constantly on the lookout for devices that I thought and hoped would make her life easier – special reading lights, magnifying devices, a new telephone book organized by categories and printed in a larger font, telephones with larger buttons, a small flashlight so she could see items in her purse.

One thing I did that worked was to thread a few needles with different colors of thread, so she would not have to struggle with that chore by herself. However, that was a small success.

Nine times out of ten, my efforts failed to improve the situation, which led to further frustration for both of us.

I realize now that <u>my</u> ideas and solutions, which made great sense to me, failed because Mom had learned to adapt more than I realized. For example, she complained extensively about being fed-up with her old, scratched–out address book, yet was unable to use the new one I made her because she navigated her way around the old one by using the same old notes and scratched-out numbers about which she complained. I did not realize that until much later.

I also wasted a lot of energy trying to convince her to use what I had created for her. After all, I <u>had</u> gone to a lot of effort – self-centeredly, I tried to make it about me. Definitely inappropriate behavior. Yet with a sense of helplessness and mounting frustration, I continued trying to find solutions to problems I could never solve.

However, with the perspective of time since her death, I now realize she knew the problems were hers to solve, and that she would find her own solutions.

While I do not know for certain, I believe Mom kept bringing problems to me because she liked the fact that I continued to try and solve them, and my ongoing efforts reassured her of my continued love and the sustained connection between the two of us. Also, she needed to vent.

QUESTIONS: Removing the Hassle from Your Loved One's Life (Yes or No)

(Please review the Table of Contents so that you can cross-reference these questions with other related chapters, for example, those in Chapter 9 - Banks, and Chapter 11 - Estate Planning.)

____ 1. Have you made an up-to-date phone list in a format that works for your loved one, not you?

____ 1a. Is it in a place where you both can find it?

____ 2. Have you included in the phone book all the numbers that are important to your loved one, whether or not the listings matter to you?

____ 3. At a minimum, do you have the names and numbers for family and for **911** prominently displayed where they can be read easily and quickly?

____ 4. Have you worked with your loved one to remove clutter from their home? *(I would caution you not to apply your definition of "clutter" arbitrarily, without first discussing the word with them. What may be clutter to you may well be treasure to them.)*

____ 5. Have you and your loved one together audited the home with an eye to simplifying/improving mobility and ease-of-access?

___ 6.   If your loved one's memory is starting to fail and he or she becomes anxious about misplacing items, have you considered and discussed removing or storing articles to help them avoid anxiety? *(While the name of such a document may vary from one state to another, have you considered asking your loved one's attorney to prepare a "List Disposing of Tangible Personal Property"? Your loved one can designate those whom they want to receive items of personal property and the list is easily updated or changed.)*

___ 7.   Do you remember how anxious you feel when you cannot find your car keys?

___ 7a. Now can you imagine how absolutely angry and frightened your loved one would be if the appliances needed to function in everyday life (false teeth, eye glasses, braces, watch, hearing aid, wedding rings, address book, portable telephone) can't be found – whether this occurs at home, in the hospital, or visiting you or a sibling?

___ 7b. Have you considered what you and your siblings can do to help your loved one retain control of various personal items for everyday living?

___ 8.   Do you or a member of your family participate in all doctor meetings and take detailed notes so you, or whomever is the primary caregiver, can review the notes and explain things later to your loved one?

____ 9.   Have you and your loved one discussed their ability to continue managing their checkbook, paying bills, and handling other routine business matters?

____ 10. Have you assumed check-writing and bill-paying responsibilities, as appropriate?

____ 11. If not, but you believe you soon will undertake banking responsibilities for your loved one, have you completed the necessary legal documents that will enable you to do so? *(Please see Chapter 9 - Banks)*

____ 12. Do you keep your loved one involved in the financial aspect of life by providing regular updates, even if they do not remember that you did so?

____ 13. Before your loved one's condition worsens to the point that you must manage their affairs, have you and your loved one discussed the current situation with their banker, attorney and financial advisor?

____ 13a. If your loved one does not want you to handle these matters, have you considered a third party designee to manage them?

____ 13b. Once your loved one's condition reaches that point, have those advisors agreed not to make major financial moves on the instruction of your loved one without calling you first? *(Please see Chapter 10 – Attorneys and consider a Durable Power of Attorney.)*

____ 13c. Have you or your loved one provided the advisors with whatever documents are needed to support this?

____ 14. If your love one's vision or hearing has diminished, have you considered providing a telephone with REALLY BIG NUMBERS or enhanced volume control? *(You may want to visit* www.JitterBug.com *and see the uncomplicated, large-format cell phones they offer for the elderly and sight-impaired.)*

____ 15. Have you created a "Key Telephone Numbers" card and placed one in your parent's wallet or purse and another in the medicine cabinet or in a clear plastic bag in the refrigerator where it could be found easily?

____ 16. Have you made or obtained duplicate keys for the home, auto and safe deposit box?

____ 16a. Are the duplicates in a safe place?

____ 17. Have you and your loved one set up specific times to call and say "hi" or check in?

____ 18. Have you considered creating a one-page monthly calendar on your computer and entering on it all upcoming activities that involve your loved one, their friends, you and other family members?

____ 18a. If so, can it be updated easily during the month?

___ 18b. Would your loved one appreciate having an extra copy to post where it can be easily seen?

___ 19. When it comes time to move your loved ones to a new home, have you considered taking photographs of the new building and grounds, as well as the new accommodations and amenities so your parents can study what will be their new home?

___ 19a. Have you encouraged your loved one to ask questions about their new home?

___ 19b. Are they having trouble envisioning how their cherished belongings will fit in a new home?

___ 19c. If so, does the proposed new home or local mover offer help such as a 'rent-a-daughter' where someone will help your loved ones figure out how much they can move with them, and where major pieces of furniture will be placed before the actual move? *(If you will Google "rent-a-daughter", you will find a number of such local organizations around the country. I have had no contact with them, and I like the concept.)*

___ 20. To help keep your loved one busy and involved as you begin to move in this direction, have you suggested that they try to figure out how best to share their special skills and talents with others? *(Something to begin thinking about is this: When it becomes time for your parent to move into new living arrangements, such as an assisted living facility or nursing home, what kinds of activities do the facilities under consideration offer residents?)* **(Please see Chapters 6 – <u>Residential Care</u> and Chapter 7 - <u>Group Family Homes</u>.)**

3
Siblings and Relatives

My comments to you: I am indebted to Larry K. for rais-ing my awareness of this dimension. As an only child, and having no relatives immediately involved when my parents died, this category was completely off my radar screen.

Since then, several friends have shared some of the difficul-ties they and their siblings have experienced as they tried to come to grips with their aging parents' deterioration, and their struggles to reach an agreement regarding the best possible care under the circumstances.

Helpful friends brought several key points to my attention. The most clearly visible common thread running through our conversations was the fact that, while the siblings loved their parents, neither siblings nor their parents discussed end-of-life situations openly and early-on. Too often there were neither written agreements nor instructions stipulating the details of what the parents wanted. Rather, there was awk-wardness and tension among all concerned and at the worst possible time.

Often siblings and parents sought to avoid upsetting each other, and so avoided talking about the ultimate reality, and in the process, upset each other even more. When things were not handled thoughtfully and empathetically, the result resembled sibling divorce™, whereby familial and sibling relationships deteriorated to such degree that the relationship resembled a divorce.

One "ah-ha!" for me was that these end-of-life issues, if not openly addressed early-on, could easily morph into multi-generational arguments, conflicts, or feuds that could take on a life of their own, cascading down from the parent to the children, to the grandchildren and perhaps beyond.

A second realization was the range of possible behind-the-scenes roles (from supportive to very divisive) that the spouses of the children and grandchildren might play in developing and implementing care plan options for the parents. There can be many stakeholders, and not all of them are either visible or obvious.

In some families, the one who spoke the loudest or had the most money steamrolled the others, and even the parent, taking control of the decision-making process, including medical treatment, the selection of a nursing home, and funeral arrangements. Rather than considering the financial realities of all concerned, that person appeared to be ego-driven, often ignoring the fact that not all the siblings had similar financial resources and disposable income to fund high-end retirement or nursing homes for their parent.

In some cases where Alzheimer's was a factor, some siblings were committed to placing their parent in a top-flight nursing home, because mom or dad was worth it. The fact that the parent might not be aware of luxurious surroundings was irrelevant.

At the other extreme, some siblings were adamant that their parent would never use Medicaid because it was beneath them, but changed their mind when confronted with the financial realities of medical expenses vs. available resources.

Ego sometimes played a role in funeral plans as well. On more than one occasion, siblings wanted to go against a parent's declared funeral wishes because they felt their parent deserved better. Further discussion sometimes yielded the admission that the sibling's reactions were face-saving because the siblings were uncomfortable or embarrassed by the wishes of their parent.

Dissimilar religious beliefs caused tension and conflict as people drew lines in the sand when they felt others were challenging, judging, disrespecting, or disregarding their beliefs.

In those cases where the siblings lived in different parts of the country, and came together only during major holidays – always a turbulent and emotional time – family members frequently *dedicated only 30 to 45 minutes to discuss plans for the needs of their parents. Often that time was interrupted by telephone calls or cut short when one or more of the siblings had to leave for some other engagement. As a result, necessary conversations and decisions occurred haphazardly, were postponed indefinitely or simply never took place.*

Before I was aware of any of the above, I thought about a four-decades-long conflict between my mother and one of her sisters. That conflict resulted in Questions 1 and 2.

And as I was thinking about Mom and her sister, I learned that a good friend of mine suffered a fatal heart attack the day before. We both were University of Maryland Terrapins, veterans, friends, business colleagues and of comparable ages, so I think of us as being connected, if not related. Questions 3 and 4 came to mind because of his death. The remaining questions resulted from my conversations. I have not faced these situations, but I have distilled the questions from my conversations, and they feel relevant to me.

QUESTIONS: Siblings and Relatives (Yes or No)

____ 1. Are you involved in any major unresolved conflicts with either your siblings or relatives that your parent would like to see resolved before he or she dies?

____ 2. Do you know if your loved one is involved in any major unresolved conflicts with relatives or friends that perhaps he or she would like to resolve before dying?

___ 3. Are there any unpaid loans or other debts that have been let slide over the years that need to be repaid, forgiven or otherwise resolved?

___ 4. If you are involved in any business dealings with siblings or relatives, have you considered making periodic reviews of existing legal and banking documents to make certain that appropriate contingencies are in place in the event of declining health or the sudden death of one of you?

___ 5. While your parent is lucid, have you, your siblings and your parent talked about the realities of the situation and come to a clear understanding of what your parent expects of each of you as their health declines?

___ 6. Even if separated geographically, have you, your siblings and your parent committed to coming together for a meeting whose sole purpose is to discuss your parent's situation?

___ 7. In the event you have all agreed to meet and one or more siblings cannot attend for whatever reason, have all of you considered granting a proxy vote to someone who will attend in the absentee's place and making a binding agreement that those absent will abide by the decisions of the rest?

___ 8.   So as to avoid the situation where those with the least financial means are forced to keep up with the siblings who have more money, have all of you considered sharing your financial conditions with each other so that everyone has a realistic understanding of how much money each person could reasonably contribute to your parent's care on an ongoing monthly basis?

___ 8a.   If that is too uncomfortable, have you considered developing a pro-rated formula to determine a contribution level that is equitable relative to the disposable income of each sibling?

___ 8b.   Does that calculation take into account your parent's ability to contribute to their own financial well-being?

___ 8c.   While your parent is lucid, have all of you discussed parental expectations and wishes for the type of retirement and nursing homes they do or do not wish to be in?

___ 9.   Have all of you considered establishing written ground rules under which all of you agree to operate when engaged in family discussions regarding the care of your parent? *(Sibling divorce™ is not acceptable.)*

_____ 10. Have all of you considered the most effective way to approach your parent in order to have the conversations you and they may have been avoiding?

_____ 10a. In those conversations, have you made certain you all have an accurate understanding of your parent's financial condition, and that you know where all important financial, family and business records are kept?

_____ 11. Have you considered taking steps to appoint one or more of your siblings as the one legally designated to handle your parent's legal affairs on behalf of all of you?

_____ 12. As all of you are interrelating, are you sensitive to each other's emotional conditions, so that one person is not dominating the conversations at the expense of others?

_____ 13. Have all of you taken into account your parent's wishes regarding the issue of Do-Not-Resuscitate (DNRs) and made certain you are able to honor their wishes? *(Please see Chapter 10 - Attorneys. Also, in Washington, Emergency Medical Technicians [EMTs] use a new HIPAA-approved document called the Physician Orders for Life-Sustaining Treatment – (POLST). You can find out additional information about it at* www.POLST.org.*)*

___ 14.   Have each of you accepted personal accountability
          to act in such a way that, in the long-term, your
          sibling relationships will not be damaged?

___ 15.   Is everyone aware of everyone else's emotional
          level so that important decisions are not made in a
          state of emotional tension or distress?

___ 16.   So as to avoid conflict, retribution and recrimi-
          nations later, have all of you and your parent
          considered talking about and making a video-
          taped or written list of mementos, keepsakes,
          heirlooms and personal treasures that your parent
          wants to give to each of you and to your children
          and friends/other relatives as well?

___ 16a. Is this information included in their will/trust?

___ 16b. Have you and your siblings, as well as your parent's
          grandchildren, identified in writing those items
          each would like to have from your parent?

___ 16c. Have all of you considered asking your parent if
          they would like the pleasure of making those gifts
          while still lucid and alive?

___ 17.   While your parent is lucid, have all of you come to
          a final, rock-solid agreement on the details of the
          funeral your parent wants you to make certain they
          receive? (*I have recently browsed through a very*

comprehensive website – www.DignityMemorial. com. *You may find it of interest as well.)*

____ 18. Are you and your siblings in agreement that, individually and collectively, you will be able to honor your parent's final wishes regarding death, their funeral and their burial? *(Please see Chapter 13 – Celebrations of Life and Burial Plans)*

____ 19. Are you and your siblings making certain that you have been sensitive to the needs of your spouses and your children as you go through this process?

____ 19a. Have you achieved a thoughtful balance between involving your children in this process so they are prepared in later life, or are you shielding them "for their own good" and perhaps denying them the chance to say good-bye? *(My father's mother was Josephine Malone Burrows and she was my favorite grandmother. I was 10 years old when she was dying. I understood the concept and I desperately wanted to see her before she died. My parents said "no" because they thought I was too young, and that seeing her on her death bed would upset me. I am 61 now. I firmly believe I would have preferred feeling whatever I would have felt vs. the long sadness of regret at not having been able to say "goodbye." I suppose I can understand my father's point of view, but his was an arbitrary decision and was the start of what I feel was a decades-long well-intended but misguided thought process.*

Years later, when Dad's prostate cancer caught up with him and he was on his death bed, my son, Chris, was visiting me. Dad forbade Mom to call me because he felt my time with Chris was more important than my seeing him before he died. She complied. And so, another arbitrary decision was made for me, for my own good, as if I were still in fifth grade and incapable of being included in making decisions that affect me. As a result, both my son and I were deprived of the opportunity to say good-bye.

Saying good-bye to my father when he was lying dead and waxy in a cardboard coffin in a hospital's cold storage room was not the same as saying good-bye when he was alive, each looking in the other's eyes and saying what each needed to say.

A teacher of mine, Patrick D., taught me that every moment is a decision, and every decision has a cost and a benefit.

I hope you will think through the ramifications of the decisions you make as you try to protect others. Please be honest. Are you really protecting others or yourself? Unknowingly, you may end up depriving them of something they need, and in the process, causing unintended hurt that may take years to heal.)

___ 20. Have you and your siblings considered that you will be setting the example for your children, because they will be watching and learning from you and someday they will be taking care of you and will bury you?

Chapter 3:
Siblings and Relatives
NOTES: SUMMARY OF "NO" POINTS

4

Finances and Insurance

*M*y *comments to you:* *Your parents or loved ones may have used the services of an accountant or a CPA (Certified Public Accountant – a professional designation granted only after passing rigorous state-controlled examinations) to prepare their taxes. As is the case with all providers of professional services, the time to get to know the accountant or CPA is while your parent is still in control of his or her mental faculties.*

I was fortunate that my CPA also handled my mother's taxes, so the preparation and filing of appropriate documents was easily achieved. I could not have managed my mother's estate without the help of my CPA and was fortunate to have had such a competent person helping me.

Please be clear: I am giving you neither legal nor financial advice. My purpose here is to raise your awareness so that you begin thinking about these issues. Because of major state and federal laws affecting both of you, and depending on the size of your parent's estate, both you and they may need significant financial and legal advice.

Tax forms will need to be filed for the year in which your parent dies. Sometimes settling the estate can take longer than you think it will. Eighteen months after Lynne's mother and stepfather died, she was still involved in settling their estate, and it was audited the following year. Keep your receipts.

For some reason, my mother's tax form 1099 from the Social Security Administration (SSA) for tax year 2002 did not arrive. The data was not available on their website, thus requiring a trip to the local SSA office. My CPA gave me the necessary documentation that enabled the SSA representative to provide me with copies of my mother's tax documents.

If you need to make the trip in person, be sure you take a certified copy of the death certificate with you, and a good book, as it may be a long wait.

Because my father had a number of years of government service, he received a pension in addition to Social Security. If that is your situation as well, you will need to provide a certified copy of the death certificate to each agency in order to stop or adjust payments in a timely manner.

Not just for the SSA, but for the many different institutions you will have to deal with, rules governing certified copies of death certificates may differ from state to state. At the price of $1.00 per copy in 2002, I purchased 15 certified copies of my mother's death certificate from the county human services department; over the course of settling her estate, I used all but two of them.

QUESTIONS: Finances & Insurance (Yes or No)

___ 1. Have you and your parents discussed their long-term personal and financial plans, including insurance, so that you understand any special issues and concerns they may have?

___ 2. Have you and your parents discussed their current financial situation, including insurance coverage, in sufficient detail that you understand their personal financial condition?

___ 3. Is there enough money to last both parents for the rest of their lives?

___ 3a. If not, are all members of the family aware of this and thinking about the need to make potential changes?

___ 4. Have you investigated any current federal, state, or county social services programs available to help them? *(Please see Appendix B - Hopeful Resources.)*

___ 5. Have you met your parents' CPA?

___ 6. Have you met their insurance agent?

___ 7. Have you, your parents and their insurance agent reviewed their insurance coverage and adjusted their policies to address their current situation and needs, as well as projected future requirements?

___ 8.   Have you and your parents considered long-term health care insurance?

___ 9.   Do you know your parents' Social Security numbers and do you have their Social Security cards in hand?

___ 9a. If not, do you know where they are?

___ 10. Do you have the contact information and account numbers for all of their pension providers?

___ 11. Do you have the contact information and account numbers for all of their insurance and medical policies?

___ 12. Upon the death of one parent, do you know whether their medical insurance will remain in force for the surviving spouse?

___ 13. Have you helped your surviving parent draw up a new budget or financial plan?

___ 14. Have you checked to see that all relevant and current insurance policies, pension statements, Healthcare Powers of Attorney, DNRs *(Please see Chapter Eight - Medical Professionals)*, bank records, Social Security cards and statements, credit cards with PIN numbers and access codes, passport, driver's license and similar documents are conveniently stored, clearly marked, well-organized and accessible?

_____ 14a. If you are the parent, does the person you want to handle your affairs for you, when the time comes, know where that information is, and can they get to it quickly and easily?

_____ 15. Are you encouraging your surviving parent to make no major financial or life decisions for at least the next six to twelve months? *(My father, Malcolm, occasionally found himself advising people who were newly-widowed or divorced. He routinely recommended they wait a year before making big decisions like selling a house, because in his experience, it took at least that long for people to begin to think clearly again. He wanted to help them avoid knee-jerk reactions that he knew they would probably later regret.)*

Chapter 4:
Finances and Insurance
NOTES: SUMMARY OF "NO" POINTS

PART II

HOME AND
HEALTH

5

Your Loved One's Home

My comments to you: Karin's parents, Konrad and Marguerite, lived in their Seattle home for over 50 years. During that time, Konrad, a frugal man and very capable but unlicensed plumber and electrician, had made a number of, shall we say, innovative upgrades to the house. Extremely independent and self-reliant, Konrad was proud of his home and all he had done there. When it came time for Karin and her brother, Richard, to sell the home, the new buyer's home inspector was intrigued with Konrad's wiring. Nonetheless, he stipulated a number of changes in order to bring the home into compliance with current building codes.

In addition to being a significant financial event, selling the family home can become an emotional one as well.

QUESTIONS: Your Loved One's Home (Yes or No)

____ 1.   Have you and your parents identified the tax consequences of selling their home?

____ 2.   Before proceeding to sell their home, have you considered visiting with the county zoning officials to learn if there are any upcoming zoning changes that may influence the value and/or the timing of the sale of their home?

___ 3. Particularly if it is an older home, before putting it on the market, have you considered hiring a licensed home inspector to identify structural issues that may be of concern to a potential buyer and also to identify existing situations that will conflict with current building code specifications?

___ 4. If the house is old and you are planning on disposing of any of the old materials in the local landfill, have you familiarized yourself with current local regulations and restrictions before taking actions that may have an environmental impact or be considered toxic? *(Rules where you live may not be the same as where a parent lives.)*

___ 5. Have you considered using the services of an Estate Agent to handle the sale of household items? *(It can take the emotional burden off your shoulders at a time when you will likely be under maximum stress. Karin retained one when she and Richard sold their parents' home and the money was well-spent. Make it easy on yourself.)*

___ 6. If you need to sell your parent's home while they are still alive, have you considered the emotional impact it may have on them?

___ 6a. Did you know that there are real estate agents who are trained and certified specialists in working with seniors? *(They are awarded the designation of Seniors Real Estate Specialist, or SRES. See www. SeniorsRealEstate.com.)*

___ 6b. If you do not need to sell the parental home after they have moved out, and if it is located in an appreciating area, have you considered renting it? *(When Karin's dad died, her mother was living in a group family home, so she and her brother, Richard, sold the house. Theirs was an emotional decision. Had they paid a property manager to rent it for them and waited a year to let things settle before making any decisions, they could have ridden the city's real estate boom market and more than doubled their money. Please do not make important decisions emotionally.)*

___ 7. Have you considered what sentimental items you want to exclude from the sale of your parents' home and take with you? *(Karin's father had been a gardener for years, and before she and Richard sold their parents' house, she took cuttings of her father's rose bushes and planted them at our home in North Carolina.*

In contrast, I read an account of a woman who sold her father's house after he died. As she left the home for the last time, she dug up her father's favorite shrub. The new owner saw her removing the plant and conflict erupted. While the situation was ultimately resolved, it could have been avoided entirely had the woman thought to exclude, in writing, the plant from the sale of the house.)

Chapter 5:
Your Loved One's Home
NOTES: SUMMARY OF "NO" POINTS

6
Residential Care

My comments to you: *Because there are so many options for residential care, it is beyond my ability to cover them all here. However, I have personal experience with residential living facilities (this chapter) and group family homes* (**Please see Chapter Seven –** **Group Family Homes***)*

My parents lived on the Gulf Coast of Florida, and after Dad died, Mom moved into a residential living facility there. She was very social and enjoyed the camaraderie among the residents of that facility and lived there for almost three years.

However, as much as Mom loved Florida, she loved family more, so she decided to move to North Carolina to be near Karin and me, as well as Jen and Chris, my two children.

At that time, Karin and I were newlyweds, and I had just moved from Cincinnati to join her in Raleigh. I moved into her house, and we subsequently bought a place of our own – a house with an unfinished basement. Shortly after we moved into our new house, Chris, my teenage son, came to live with us. Hard on the heels of that transition, Mom said she would like to pay for finishing the basement and move in as well.

With more than a little trepidation, Karin and I agreed, but before the sheetrock went up, Mom made some comments that made us realize that it would not work – too many people, too soon in a new marriage and new home. We pulled the plug. Mom took the news graciously.

After Chris settled in, Mom reopened the topic, and this time she moved to a nearby apartment complex. For the next year, an interesting transformation took place, one that may have application for you and your parent.

Mom lived three miles from us. The residents were mostly young families. The young parents and their children energized her. We saw her frequently and were pleased to see that she adapted well to her new surroundings.

However, because Mom enjoyed socializing and making friends in the complex, she became ever more upset and lonely as residents she had just gotten to know moved on to their first houses or to other jobs. Her loneliness and the need to be with people her own age became her ongoing preoccupation. And so we began looking for a residential living facility comparable to where she had lived in Florida.

QUESTIONS: Residential Care (Yes or No)
(*Please see Chapter Seven: <u>Group Family Homes</u>*)

____ 1.   Have you discussed at all with your parents what they want to do as their next step?

___ 1a. If so, what options have you discussed? _____

_____

_____

___ 2. Have you and your parents agreed that you will begin looking for a retirement home at the first sign of approaching need rather than waiting until the need is urgent?

___ 3. Have you determined how the residential living facility handles administrative matters and Medicare/Medicaid?

___ 3a. Do you know the differences between Medicare and Medicaid? *(Both are medical care programs under the direction of the U.S. Department of Health and Human Services.* **Medicare** *is a federally administered program providing medical care for people age 65 and over.* **Medicaid** *provides medical care for the needy; it is a joint federal/state program administered by the states, under federal guidelines. According to this website –* www.medicare.gov/Publications/Pubs/pdf/11034.pdf *– "Under limited conditions, Medicare will pay some nursing home costs such as when a patient needs skilled nursing or rehabilitation services after a hospital stay. For more information, call your local State Health Insurance Assistance Program or Nursing Home Ombudsman – see* www.aoa.gov."

It goes on to state that "Medicaid is a state and federal program that will pay most nursing home costs for people with limited income and resources. Eligibility varies by state. Medicaid will pay for nursing home care only when provided in a Medicaid-certified facility. For information about Medicaid eligibility, call your ... State Medical Assistance office – 1.800. MEDICARE or 1.800.633.4227 – for the telephone number in your area.")

_____ 4. Do you know what will happen if your parent requires extra care that needs to be provided through private or supplemental insurance?

_____ 5. Do you have a clear understanding of the "fine print" in the admissions contract, particularly about what the residential living facility is obligated to do regarding the provision of long-term medical care?

_____ 6. Do you know if admission is contingent upon passing certain physical and mental tests?

_____ 6a. If so, would it be advisable to take the tests sooner rather than later?

_____ 7. If your parent wants to change units, do you know if the management charges special fees?

_____ 8. If your parent wants to change units, will management move your parent or will that be up to you?

___ 9. In addition to monthly rent, does the facility charge a large, up-front entrance fee that is pro-rated and refundable over a multi-year time frame? *(Not all residential living facilities require this fee. Some simply charge a modest initial fee and monthly rent. Please inquire about the conditions and procedures that may govern pro-rated refunds of fees if your parent moves out or dies before the end of the contract period. Get it in writing.)*

___ 10. Have you identified all of the services that the facility provides?

___ 10a. Do you know which of those services are included in the monthly rent and which are extra?

___ 11. Do you know how much storage space is provided and how personal goods are secured?

___ 12. Are there any additional monthly expenses for which you or your parent will be responsible?

___ 13. Is the facility certified, licensed, bonded or accredited?

___ 13a. If it is, by whom? *(It is important to know this because when the facility is certified, licensed, bonded or accredited, it is more likely to provide better care for your parent.)*

___ 13b. Is the facility's business license clearly posted, perhaps near the entrance, and is it up-to-date?

_____ 13c. If the State allows for several levels or types of licenses, is that stated on the license?

_____ 14. Do you know what transportation services the residential living facility provides to take residents to churches, community centers, libraries, doctors, recreational outings, shopping and to other outside activities?

_____ 14a. Have you and your parent sat and ridden in the vehicles they use to transport residents?

_____ 14b. Were they comfortable?

_____ 14c. Could your parent get into and out of them without difficulty?

_____ 14d. Does the home's insurance coverage extend to residents when they are riding in such vehicles?

_____ 14e. If it does not, are you and your parent certain that their own insurance policy will cover them as passengers traveling in the residential facility's vehicles?

_____ 14f. Can your parent have their own automobile at the facility? Under what conditions?

_____ 15. Do any of their residents utilize the services of a computerized emergency response company? (Such services provide an activation device on a necklace or wristwatch that summons help when the wearer pushes a button.)

___ 16. Do you know which home health care services the facility is affiliated with, i.e. Visiting Nurses, United Way, Elder Care Support Services, the local Council on Aging, Hospice or any local adult day care centers?

___ 17. Have you and your parent personally met with the facility's management staff?

___ 17a. Did you like what you saw?

___ 17b. Did your parent like the management?

___ 18. When you and your parent met with the management of the facility, did you ask about:

___ 18a. rate of turnover among management and staff?

___ 18b. levels of training among management and staff?

___ 18c. whether staff members are routinely expected to work overtime / double shifts?

___ 18d. educational certifications held by management?

___ 18e. frequency of visits by physical therapy specialists?

___ 18f. the average age of the residents?

___ 18g. the interests of the residents and activities that are planned for them?

___ 19. Did you and your parent meet the in-house physician?

_____ 19a. Did you and your parent interview that physician?

_____ 19b. Do you know the doctor's professional credentials?

_____ 19c. Did you and your parent like the doctor?

_____ 20. Did you and your parent tour the facility and see the range of living quarters and medical care facilities?

_____ 20a. Did you and your parent eat more than one meal in the dining facility?

_____ 20b. Did you both like the food?

_____ 20c. Were the members of the dining room staff friendly, polite and competent?

_____ 20d. Did any of the residents greet your parent?

_____ 21. Were all of the living areas and common activities areas clean?

_____ 21a. Did the facility smell clean and fresh, or not?

_____ 21b. Were the carpets clean, or were they stained?

_____ 22. Were residents left sitting in the hallways, strapped to chairs, alone and unattended?

_____ 22a. Was there any evidence of "accidents" that had not been cleaned up at once?

_____ 23. When your parent becomes so infirm that he or she can no longer live independently, are you absolutely clear (*in writing*) about whether or not the facility will be responsible for providing continual long-term care there on-site?

____ 23a. Or, if they have no long-term care available on-site, does the fine print in the contract permit them to send your parent to another facility?

____ 23b. Do you know if there are time parameters around this situation?

____ 23c. If they could be sent to other facilities, do you know which ones and have you checked them out?

____ 24. Have you verified that the residence is properly insured and fiscally sound?

____ 24a. Do you know what options may be available to you and your parent if the facility goes bankrupt?

____ 25. Did you speak privately with a sampling of the current residents to see what they think of the treatment they have received?

____ 26. Have you asked what happens if your parent runs out of money?

____ 26a. If you and your parent are interested in the facility, have you considered asking the facility management to include the answer to that question in the residential contract, if it is not there already?

___ 26b. Before committing, do you want to run the contract by either your or your parent's attorney?

___ 27. Have you considered checking with the local newspapers to see if they have run any adverse stories about the facility?

___ 28. Did your parent like the facility and the people?

___ 28a. Did your parents think they would be happy there?

___ 28b. Would you be happy having your parent there?

Chapter 6:
Residential Care
NOTES: SUMMARY OF "NO" POINTS

_____

_____

_____

_____

_____

_____

_____

_____

_____

_____

_____

_____

_____

_____

_____

_____

_____

_____

_____

_____

_____

_____

7

Group Family Homes

My **comments to you:** *Because Karin's mom, Marguerite, had some health-care issues that required special attention when her health began to fail, Karin and I spent a lot of time and energy visiting a number of group family homes. Ultimately, we found one that – from our perspective – was perfect for her. Marguerite seemed to like the home, the staff and the owner so we enrolled her.*

If your and your parent's situation permits, the ideal situation would be to actively involve him or her in the selection process and visit as many facilities as possible.

I only learned of this resource while writing this book; perhaps it will be of help to you. If you go to www.Medicare.gov and scroll down to "Search Tools" and highlight "Compare Nursing Homes in Your Area," you should find an enormous amount of comparative data.

A word of caution: it is possible that your parent will not share your enthusiasm, no matter how fine the facility or how much effort you have gone through to find it. If this happens, try not to take it personally.

With hindsight, while Karin and I were sensitive to Marguerite's losses – first of her home and then of Konrad – and were grieving ourselves, I realize now that we did not fully comprehend the magnitude of the personal impact that these two huge life transitions had on her.

Suddenly, the roles of parent and child were reversed, and they may well be for you too.

QUESTIONS: Group Family Homes (Yes or No)
(Please also see Chapter Six - Residential Care)

____ 1.   Is the facility certified, licensed, bonded or accredited?

____ 1a.   If so, by whom? *(It is important to know this because when the facility is certified, licensed, bonded or accredited, it means the likelihood of better care for your parent.)*

____ 2.   When you first enter the facility, does it smell clean and fresh? *(If it smells bad, do not waste your time – just leave.)*

____ 2a.   Have you and your parent personally visited and inspected the home in the morning, afternoon, evening and at bedtime?

____ 3.   Have you and your parent sampled all three meals?

____ 4.   During your visits, were you and your parent impressed with the way the staff and residents interacted with each other as well as how management interacted with the staff and residents?

____ 5. Have you and your parent had a face-to-face meeting with the facility manager?

____ 5a. Were all of your parent's and your questions answered to your complete satisfaction?

____ 6. Did you get a generally good feeling about how the home is run?

____ 7. Have you talked with the residents about the frequency, variation and quality of recreational events?

____ 8. Were you and your parent invited to attend one of the recreational events at the facility?

____ 9. When disagreements occur between residents, do you and your parent know how management resolves them?

____ 10. Did a manager or staff member give you a complete tour of the facility?

____ 10a. Did the manager greet residents by name and interact with them in a non-condescending manner?

____ 11. Were you invited/permitted to walk the facility by yourself? *(This is important because the residents may be more forthcoming with you when a member of staff is not present.)*

____ 12. Did the residents appear happy and well-cared-for?

____ 13. Did you see any residents sitting by themselves in a hallway, strapped to a chair, perhaps with a puddle under the chair?

____ 14. Were the carpets clean and the floors polished?

____ 15. Were residents being ignored in any way?

____ 16. Did your parent like the residents? Did he or she feel they had enough in common with the residents to enjoy living there?

____ 16a. Do you know the average age of the other residents?

____ 16b. While maintaining resident confidentiality, do you know the medical conditions of the other residents? *(This may be important because at least one major newspaper has reported a growing national trend, at least in nursing homes, where they accept younger residents for whom old age is not a problem but who may have other medical, substance or psychiatric issues.)*

____ 17. Before making the final decision, have you spoken with family members of other residents to gain their perspectives about the facility and of the care their family member is receiving?

____ 17a. Have you and your parent met with the cooks and cleaning staff?

_____ 17b. Do you or your parent envision any communication problems?

_____ 18. Have you verified with external sources that the facility is adequately insured? *(Insurance requirements vary by state. At this time in my state, there is no law requiring group homes to carry liability coverage. Because the insurance industry here has experienced some large losses, they have raised their premiums significantly. Consequently, many owners of group family homes have dropped their liability coverage and have reorganized their legal structure so as to limit their legal and financial exposure.)*

_____ 19. Have you considered discussing with the manager your desire to situate your parent only in a group family home that is financially stable and asked the manager how he or she can best put your concerns to rest? *(I know questions such as these may feel uncomfortable. Ask them anyway; these are your parents we are talking about here. The management of a professionally-run group family home should be able to answer them forthrightly.)*

_____ 20. Have you thought about calling the Better Business Bureau to see if they have received any complaints about the facility?

_____ 21. Have you considered contacting the local newspaper to see if they have run any stories (either

positive or negative) about the facility or are currently conducting any investigations about them?

___ 22. Have you asked to review management's safety
and security procedures?

___ 22a. Have you determined that they are up-to-date, ad-
equate, and effective to meet your parent's physical
and psychological needs as well as yours?

___ 23. If your parent needs routine medical treatment
off-site, do you know that their treatment would
be handled appropriately?

___ 24. Have you asked what routine medical treatments
are available in the facility?

___ 25. Do you know which medical treatments they are
licensed to provide on-site?

___ 26. If your parent needs help using the bathroom at
night, do you know how the assistance would be
provided?

___ 27. Do you know if your parent's insurance will pay
for treatments at the group family home? *(Please
see Chapter Four - Finances & Insurance)*

___ 28. Do you know which insurance carriers the home
works with?

___ 29. Do you and your parent have a clear understanding what personal items can be brought if the parent enters this home?

___ 30. Do you and your parent know how the management handles trips outside such as to the barber shop, beauty parlor or doctor appointments?

___ 31. Do you know if your parent can have money with them?

___ 31a. If yes, how is it handled? _____
If they cannot, why not? _____

___ 31b. Do you know how they address residents' need for cash for everyday expenses?

___ 32. If your parent's condition worsens, do you know what procedures are in place to insure that proper medical care is provided?

___ 33. Do you know if the group family home is approved for payment by Medicare and/or Medicaid? *(Please see Chapter Six – Residential Care)*

___ 34. Have you asked the management of the group family home by what percent have monthly payments increased over the last two years?

___ 34a. Is another increase expected in the near future?

___ 35. Do you know if pets are allowed in the facility? If so, what are the restrictions?

___ 36. Does your parent have any allergies that would be aggravated by pets of other residents?

____ 37. Do you know how the manager recruits, screens, hires and trains the caregivers?

____ 38. Have you considered asking the manager if any of the current employees have been terminated from other facilities for reasons that would concern either you or your parent?

____ 39. Have you considered asking the manager to explain to you the recruiting, reference-checking and hiring processes used to screen out applicants with prior criminal convictions?

____ 40. Have you asked the manager for references so you can check his/her education and areas of special expertise?

____ 41. Do you know how long the manager has worked at that group family home?

____ 41a. In the industry?

____ 42. If you were going to be the resident, would you want to live there?

____ 43. If the facility meets your criteria, what does your parent think of it?

____ 44. If your parent's reaction is negative, have you considered ways to make it positive?

____ 45. If everything passes muster, have you asked your parent if he or she wants to move in?

Chapter 7:
Group Family Homes
NOTES: SUMMARY OF "NO" POINTS

8

Medical Professionals

My comments to you: Karin and I could not have been more fortunate with the physicians who provided primary care for our parents in the final years of their lives. In addition to competency, the overriding universal trait that all three physicians shared was an unwavering commitment to treat each of our parents not as patients but rather as unique individuals.

None of them ever talked down to our parents or patronizingly called them "dear," as often happens to the elderly, or worse, spoke about them as if they were not even in the room.

*The Golden Rule states "Treat others the way you want to be treated." Each of our parents' physicians applied the **Platinum Rule**. **They treated each parent as that parent wanted to be treated.** If you can find physicians who apply the Platinum Rule, hang on to them with both hands because you and your parents will be more tranquil and much happier.*

On a related note, in my experience, one caregiver that often goes unsung is the pharmacist. Mom was fortunate to have found a fine one, a woman who was competent, caring, and compassionate. She did not just fill pill orders. She actively paid attention to what the doctor was prescribing. She went out of her way to take care of Mom when I was traveling, and was unfailingly willing to spend time with her. We both looked forward to our trips to that pharmacy.

Questions: Medical Professionals (Yes or No)

____ 1.   Does the doctor take a holistic approach to caring by paying attention to your parent's mental, spiritual, and emotional condition, as well as his or her physical condition? *(I was fortunate in finding a holistically-oriented family doctor when we lived in North Carolina, and even more fortunate that Mom liked and trusted her as well.)*

____ 1a.   Does your parent complain about her physical condition to you but tell the doctor she feels fine? *(This was an on-going frustration for me, and I was able to resolve it with some straight talk with Mom and with the help of our fine family physician in North Carolina.)*

____ 2.   Have you made it a point to become known to your loved one's physicians, dentist and pharmacist?

____ 3.   If you call your parent's doctor, will the administrative staff and the doctor's nurse know who you are?

___ 4.   Are you paying sufficient attention to your parent's condition so that you would notice any changes in behavior indicating the onset of problems, such as depression or Alzheimer's?

___ 5.   Do you have a calendar or daily record devoted to your parent's medical information?

___ 6.   Have you considered what important data and documents you would want to have with you at all times? *(I use a planner and devoted one section to Mom's medical records and related legal documents. This was particularly helpful when I was called to the ER in the early hours of the morning, which happened more than once. Do you have something similar?*

Here are the items I kept in my planner for Mom:
- *My notes from doctor visits from the preceding 12 months, including blood pressure and copies of test results*
- *Current list of all medications, including prescription numbers; pharmacy phone number, dosage and schedule*
- *List of past illnesses and operations (with dates)*
- *Social Security number*
- *Insurance information*
- *Telephone numbers for doctors, dentist, hospital and ambulance*
- *Blood type*

- *Photocopy of her driver's license and*
- *List of allergies and medications to which she was allergic*

Mom was not an organ donor, nor had she made burial plans, but if she had, I would have had that information on hand as well. I also had these legal documents: Do Not Resuscitate (also known as a DNR), Living Will, and Healthcare Power of Attorney. **Please see Chapter Ten – <u>Attorneys</u>.**

As an aside, I have recently had eye-opening conversations with physicians who said that, even if a patient has a valid DNR, they feel it is up to their professional discretion whether they will accept it, or will take steps to resuscitate the patient in spite of the DNR. It seems to me to be a topic worthy of discussion with your parent and their physician.)

____ 7. Do you keep a dated, written record of all of your parent's medical complaints, concerns or questions so you are prepared for meetings with the physician?

____ 8. Do you have a written record of all the diseases and ultimate causes of death of as many blood relatives as possible? *(I hope this does not sound morbid. The more information you can provide your parent's physicians, the more effective the treatment will be. Safeguard this information as it will become important to you as you age.)*

___ 9. When you and your parent meet with their doctor, do you keep a detailed record of that visit so you can review with him or her what was discussed and agreed upon, as well as any changes of medications?

___ 10. Are you aware of all of your parent's health-related appointments?

___ 11. Have you considered helping your parent keep a log of daily physical, mental and emotional conditions, or considered keeping it for them?

___ 12. Have you helped your parent prepare a weekly pill chart? (*The one I made for Mom was a simple table prepared in Microsoft Word. I put the date and the days of the week across the top and a list of her medications down the left side. Even after her first stroke and subsequent TIAs, she kept her own records, right up to the end. I filled her pill boxes each week and periodically double-checked both her medications and the chart.)*

___ 13. Do you frequently check the pill chart and the contents of the pill box to be sure the chart is being filled in accurately and that the count of pills provided and taken match?

_____ 14. Do you know your parent's pharmacist?

_____ 15. Has your parent signed all pertinent compliance documents for the **Health Insurance Portability and Accountability Act of 1996 (HIPAA)** so the physician and the hospital can legally share all of your parent's medical information with you? *(Do not ignore this. Unless all the appropriate documents are signed and current, hospitals and doctors will not share information with you. Period. When your parent signs the HIPAA documents for the first time, it would be a good idea to ask when they will need to re-sign the authorization forms. Plan accordingly.)*

_____ 16. Have you identified and met three physicians who are familiar with your parent's physical and mental condition and who would be willing to testify in court if necessary? *(This is important, because if or when your parent becomes mentally or physically unable to care for himself or herself, you may be required to provide three qualified independent medical specialists to confirm that your parent is "unable to make rational personal decisions," or that his or her "mental competency is in question." If that situation arises, you will want to be able to take appropriate legal action in a timely manner. Please seek legal advice.)*

___ 17. With your parent's permission, have you made copies for yourself of their medical records?

___ 18. Is there a private local ambulance service for which you can enroll your parent? *(It was very touching to me that, even after Mom had her strokes and her memory sometimes lapsed, one bill she always remembered to make sure I paid was for the ambulance service. I am sure it was something Dad told her to always keep in force.)*

Chapter 8:
Medical Professionals
NOTES: SUMMARY OF "NO" POINTS

PART III

TAKING CARE OF BUSINESS

9

Banks

My comments to you: Being conservative institutions, banks take seriously their mandate to protect their customers' money. Before getting into the topic, I am going to take a slight detour to a related issue.

Both of my parents fit the profile of a conservative banker. Being frugal and financially conservative, they created an estate plan while both were healthy and still able to do so. That estate plan included a structured financial plan containing all of their joint assets.

Prior to his death, Dad made certain that all their assets, including the house, car, checking and savings accounts, were protected by placing each of their assets in a trust. Upon the death of one spouse, the assets would pass, with no tax consequences, to the surviving spouse.

Upon Dad's death, Mom and I met with their trust attorney in Florida and created a new trust between the two of us. Because trust laws differ from state to state, when Mom moved up from Florida, we went to a North Carolina trust at-

torney, revoked the Florida trust and created one that would be legal in North Carolina.

Please do not ignore the issue of trusts. Doing so would likely be penny-wise and pound-foolish. Whatever it costs – within reason – it will pay dividends in the long run.

Because Mom and Dad made sure I understood that bank accounts should be protected by a trust, I have included their thoughts here. *(Please see Chapter 10 – Trusts and Wills.)*

Getting back to the issue of banks, my experience has been that bankers are ethical and will not share privileged information regarding their customers with people who suddenly appear, claiming to be family members but are unknown to the bank staff.

If your parent's particular situation permits, it will be of significant benefit to you both to meet the banker while your parent is still ambulatory and in control of his mental faculties. If your parent has not already added you to their safe deposit box and checking and savings accounts, the time to be added, and thereby become known to the banking staff, is **before** the need arises.

On a related note, Mom taught me first-hand that a checkbook is a very personal document, and the keeping of it can be a source of pride and independence to an elderly person. She kept her own checkbook up to the time of her first serious stroke.

When it was clear to me that both her vision and her cognitive skills were impaired, it became necessary for me to assume responsibility for paying her bills and managing her checkbook. She took great exception to my assessment.

Rather than arbitrarily taking it from her, I got a couple of bills and her calculator and asked her to pay them. I stepped away so she was not under scrutiny and when I returned, she was both furious and in tears. She admitted she could not see clearly, had lost the manual dexterity to write in the proper columns, could not fill in either check properly, or push the right buttons on the calculator. After that, the transfer, while sad, was smooth.

My lesson: the transition was much easier because **Mom had proven to herself** *that she was unable to do it. While stressful for us both, I believe that handling the situation that way was much less damaging to her than if I had arbitrarily taken the checkbook from her. This may have been a subtle distinction, but it was crucial to our ongoing relationship.*

Realizing she still wanted to be involved, I reviewed the bills I was paying and kept her updated on the status of her finances.

My suggestion: talk with your parent about future crossroads you both know are coming and consider establishing some ground rules to deal with them. One such ground rule might be to have your parent or loved one display competency in doing *a task, like paying bills. Then, when you come to a crossroads situation, rather than risking becoming combative, and perhaps bullying, refer back to your earlier agreement and ask your parent to demonstrate competency. If she can do the task, peachy! And if not, gently remind her of the ground rules. This may work, or it may not. If it does, it may save you both a lot of anguish. (**Please see Chapter 9 - __Attorneys__** for another example, this one involving drivers licenses.)*

QUESTIONS: Banking (Yes or No)

____ 1. Do you know the locations and account numbers for all banks where your parent has accounts?

____ 1a. If your parent has credit or debit cards linked to these accounts, do you know the PIN numbers and answers to whatever security questions may be in place?

____ 2. Has your parent introduced you to the bank manager, head teller and staff in each bank where she does business?

____ 2a. Has she made it clear that, when the time comes, you are authorized to handle their banking business for her?

____ 3. Have you provided the bank with whatever legal and procedural documents they require?

____ 4. If appropriate, has your parent complied with bank procedures to add you to existing accounts?

____ 4a.   Have you asked the bank manager and your attorney about any potential liabilities of having someone else on your account?

____ 5.   Have you and your parent considered what type of legal rights you will have on the account? *(If you are a <u>co-signer</u>, you will be able to sign checks with your parent. If you are a <u>co-owner with right of survivorship</u>, the account will transfer immediately to you upon the death of your parent. Please be sure to discuss options and implications with your parent's banker, their attorney and your tax advisor if appropriate. To expedite the transition of the account from your parent to you, you may need to provide the banker with the appropriate documents.)*

____ 6.   Have you and your parent considered which additional family members, if any, are to be on the bank accounts and/or have access to their safe deposit box?

____ 7.   In addition to savings and checking accounts, does your parent have more than one safe deposit box?

____ 7a.   Do you know where each box is located?

____ 7b.   Do you have signing access to enter the box(es)?

____ 7c.   Do you know where your parent keeps the keys to the box(es)?

____ 7d. Have you and your parent determined which documents should be stored in the box and which should be stored at home?

____ 8. Have you and your parent inventoried the contents of each box?

____ 8a. Have you made certain to keep a copy of the inventory someplace other than locked up in the box?

____ 9. After your parent dies, do you know if you will have immediate access to their safe deposit box, or will the bank seal it pending future legal proceedings?

____ 10. If your parents have a trust, have they determined with their banker and their trust attorney which assets should be placed in the trust?

____ 11. Do you and your parents want to review all accounts and consider closing any that it makes sense to close?

____ 12. At the time when your parents are unable to manage their banking themselves, and before you assume responsibility and control of their accounts, do you know if all the bank paperwork is in order for you to do so?

Chapter 9:
Banks
NOTES: SUMMARY OF "NO" POINTS

10
Attorneys

My comments to you: *At the risk of boring you with re-peated disclaimers, I want to reiterate that I am sharing what I have learned from my experiences; I am* not *providing you with legal advice. That is what attorneys are for. Please consult an attorney on all legal matters relevant to managing your parents' affairs.*

As with bankers, the time to get to know your parents' attorney, if they have one, is while your parents are alive and well.

Because a number of legal instruments needed to be created, I was not competent to make recommendations to Mom. However, I was capable of spending a lot of time talking with her to help her think through and clarify her desires, so that when we went to her trust attorneys in Florida and North Carolina, who were definitely "on the clock," she was prepared to make effective use of their time and her money.

This was important for three reasons. First, like many people who lived through the Depression, she had a fear of outliving her money. Second, because she was an innate skeptic, she wanted to be certain that her attorney would not take advantage of her. Third and most important, because she felt a great sense of accountability to be an effective steward of what money she and Dad had earned, she wanted to be certain she managed it as Dad would have wanted.

If it is necessary to make changes to wills and trust documents, request a meeting for you and your parent with the attorney. When Mom and I met with her Florida and North Carolina trust attorneys, each spent a good deal of time with us together to guarantee that they understood our wishes. Both times, when we were done, each asked me to leave the room so he could confirm with Mom, without my being present to influence her, that what she had said with me in the room was indeed what she wanted.

If your attorney asks you to leave the room, please do not take it personally; it is a mark of professionalism.

QUESTIONS: Attorneys (Yes or No)

____ 1.   Do you feel comfortable that you and your parent have discussed their wishes in enough detail that you know their desires?

____ 2.   Do your parents have a will?

____ 2a.   Is it current and can they lay their hands on it? *(A **will** is a legal document that spells out what you want to have happen after you die. The will should* *appoint someone to carry out your last wishes. If you have young children, it should name a guardian for them. It should clearly spell out who gets what. You can also address things like funeral arrangements, who gets your pets, organ donation and charitable donations. Some assets, like life insurance policies, IRAs, 401(k) retirement plans and bank accounts typically have beneficiaries that fall beyond the scope of your will, so be sure to keep them up-to-date. For the will to be valid, you must sign and date it in front of at least two disinterested parties, witnesses who stand to gain nothing from you or your estate.)*

_____ 3.   Do you know if your parents have a trust attorney?

_____ 3a. Are you known to the attorney and his or her administrative staff?

_____ 4.   Do you have a complete and up-to-date contact list of any other attorneys your parent currently uses?

_____ 5.   Is it time to schedule another meeting with the attorney(s)?

_____ 6.   Have you confirmed that the attorneys understand and support, not only your parent's current needs and financial expectations, but also yours for the future?

____ 7. Have you, your parent and the attorney discussed and resolved all necessary trust requirements and created the appropriate instruments?

____ 7a. Is it time for you and your parent to revisit the trust plan?

____ 8. If you are named as beneficiary upon the death of your parent, do the current legal instruments you and they have in place create an unfavorable legal/tax burden for you?

____ 9. Do you and/or your parent have the appropriate current legal documents, recognized in both your home state and theirs, in effect? Among these instruments are:

____ 9a. **Durable Power of Attorney?** *(This instrument grants someone else the legal authority to make decisions for you in the event that you are unable to make them for yourself.)*

____ 9b. **Durable Health Care Power of Attorney?** *(This instrument grants someone else the legal authority to make medical decisions for you in the event you are unable to make them for yourself.)*

____ 9c. **Living Will or Health Care Directive?** *(A Living Will communicates to medical professionals your wishes regarding the circumstances under which you do not wish to be kept alive. A Health Care*

Directive sets forth the medical procedures you do and do not wish to have done to you in order to be kept alive.)

____ 9d. **Do Not Resuscitate (DNR)?** _(An order telling medical professionals not to perform cardiopulmonary resuscitation – CPR.)_

____ 9e. **Last Will and Testament?** _(Tells how the estate is to be distributed when the time comes. It is often linked to a Trust.)_

____ 9f. **Living Trust?** _(A Living Trust is used to transfer things of value, i.e. stocks, bonds, real estate, personal possessions from one living person to another. Properly created and executed, it enables an estate to avoid probate. If the person who creates the trust makes it revocable, it can be changed or cancelled.)_

As you can see, there are a lot of legal items to consider. Because laws vary from state to state, it is imperative that you seek competent professional legal help to create custom documents that will serve both you and your parent. You may need current and properly-executed copies of these documents for banks and others as needed.

Please see The Parent Care Conversation _by Dan Taylor for a complete review of these and other legal instruments.)_

_____ 10. If your parent lives out-of-state, have you considered checking with a physician in your home state to make certain that the parent's DNR will be valid in your state if the parent comes to visit or live near or with you?

_____ 11. Are all documents clearly worded and free of ambiguity? *(Please see **Chapter 12 – Investment Advisors** – to make certain any existing powers of attorney and healthcare powers of attorney compliment existing trust documents.)*

_____ 12. If your parent is living with you and you are or will incur expenses as a result, (i.e. installation of grab bars in the bathroom, or carpet cleaning as needed), have you considered keeping copies of all receipts for all expenses incurred as a result of their being with you? *(Please check with both CPA and trust attorney to determine if you can ask the estate to reimburse these expenses.)*

_____ 13. Will your parents' documents, as written, enable their estate to avoid probate when they die? *(Probate is the legal establishment of the validity of someone's will. It is handled through the courts and can be both time-consuming and costly. Probate laws vary by state, so again, please seek competent professional help in the appropriate jurisdiction. Know that estate planning attorneys are not always pro-*

bate attorneys. Both are highly specialized fields, so do seek competent professional legal help. Perhaps I sound like a broken record, but this is too important to just brush over.)

_____ 14. Has your parent left a copy of the DNR, current medications and medical instructions in a plastic bag in the refrigerator?

_____ 14a. If so, is there a clearly-marked sign on the refrigerator door? *(Regardless of how odd this may sound, it was standard practice in both residential living facilities where Mom lived. Local emergency medical personnel, when they came to take someone to the hospital, would always check the refrigerator for special instructions before giving any medications. In my state, emergency medical personnel are using a new form, more detailed than the DNR. It is called a Physician Orders for Life-Sustaining Treatment (POLST.) Here is the link: www.wsma.org/patients/polst.html.)*

_____ 15. Have you considered giving your parent's attorney the names, account numbers, addresses and phone numbers for all of your parent's investment accounts?

_____ 16. Have you and your parent considered introducing his or her CPA/accountant, banker, financial advisor and attorney to each other so they can work together on your parent's behalf?

_____ 17.   Have you considered the best way to title your parents vehicle(s), particularly if their health is failing and they continue to drive? *(If a parent is involved in — or is the cause of — an accident, your name on the title could involve you in a lawsuit.*

It is important to pay attention to the details of a parent or loved one's behavior so that you can tell when that person's health is beginning to fail, and they become unsafe to themselves and to others. I saw Mom about five times a week and paid close attention to her physical, mental and emotional states. It was easy to see when she began to decline.

She was very pleased that the North Carolina Department of Motor Vehicles had renewed her license for another 10 years and was quite flip about saying that she would not be around for another renewal. She fully intended to drive for as long as SHE wanted to. However, after her stroke, her reflexes diminished greatly and her vision would come and go.

I was on the title with her and could also be held financially libel if she hit someone or damaged personal property. In short, she could no longer drive her car and it would have been irresponsible of me to let her.

It fell to me to tell her so, and the conversation broke Mom's heart, for two reasons, one obvious and one not. The first and more obvious one had to do with losing her independence. The second one was more subtle and was the real reason. The car was Mom's last tangible link to Dad and the wonderful road trips they had taken together.

It took a while to figure that out because both of us were focusing on the past, and loss – Mom losing her independence and me losing more of my time as her dependence on me increased. We went back and forth, getting both angrier and nowhere.

*Recalling the checkbook incident (**Please see Chapter 9 – Banks**), I suggested we go for a test drive. I drove her to an empty parking lot and we changed places. I asked Mom to drive along at a reasonable speed, and told her that at some point I was going to shout "stop," as if I saw a child about to run in front of the car. I wanted us both to see how long it took her to react and bring the car safely to a stop.*

After the third failure, she acknowledged that both her reflexes and her vision were such that she should no longer drive, and she gave me her car keys.

Chapter 10:
Attorneys
NOTES: SUMMARY OF "NO" POINTS

11
Estate Planning

*M*y **comments to you:** *As I have stated several times, I am not an attorney, so please make absolutely certain you seek expert legal advice from a knowledgeable specialist before you and your parent make any final estate planning decisions. Do not, under any circumstances, be penny-wise and pound-foolish in this area, as you could all pay the penalty many times over.*

As I said, my parents wanted to avoid probate. Joy Loverde, author of The Complete Eldercare Planner, *defines probate as "the process of identifying and paying heirs, creditors and determining taxes."*

Mom and Dad feared probate because they knew it could drag on for months and be very expensive. Trust attorneys, while not cheap, are a bargain when compared with what can happen in probate. Mom willingly paid their fees, and enjoyed the peace-of-mind that came with having legal documents that she knew were properly drafted and executed. Upon Mom's death, our trust attorney coordinated the distribution of Mom's assets according to her wishes in a very straightforward and rapid manner.

No matter what your or your loved one's financial situation, please do not make the mistake of thinking there is no need to consider estate planning. If you or your loved one or your parents have assets to be passed on, then you each owe it to all concerned to investigate what appropriate estate-planning resources are available.

QUESTIONS: Estate-Planning (Yes or No)

_____ 1. Are you and your parent in agreement that you want to avoid probate?

_____ 1a. Does the estate-planning attorney understand and support the desire?

_____ 2. If your parent or parents have an estate plan that was drawn up years ago, have you and they reviewed it to make certain it still reflects their current situation and wishes?

_____ 3. Is the person designated as the trustee or executor still the most appropriate person for that role? *(The <u>trustee</u> is responsible for managing the trust; the <u>executor</u> makes certain that the provisions of the will are carried out, and also sees to it that all expenses, taxes, and debts are paid.)*

_____ 3a. If not, have you and your parent taken steps with your trust attorney to make the necessary changes as quickly and smoothly as possible?

____ 4.   Do your parents' current documents clearly define what is to happen if either or both of them are unable to make rational decisions for themselves and others?

____ 5.   Have you made certain the documents are written so that either parent can change them if the other is deemed mentally incompetent?

____ 6.   If the current documents were prepared by a trust specialist (a member of American College of Trusts and Estate Counsel – *www.actec.org*) and changes need to be made to reflect the current situation, new beneficiaries, or other key changes, have you considered that the best person to amend the trust may be the trust attorney who first drew it up?

____ 7.   If you need an estate-planning attorney, is that person certified as a specialist by the state bar association? *(Note that not all estate planning attorneys specialize in trust planning and have expertise in the laws that govern them.)*

____ 8.   Have you and your parents considered moving <u>all</u> assets from their individual names and placing them into the Trust(s)?

____ 9.   Have you and your parent discussed with their trust attorney whether or not it is necessary to create a new Power of Attorney or a new Will?

____ 10. Have you confirmed that the wording in the governing documents regarding the distribution of funds upon the death of one spouse will suit the needs of the surviving parent?

____ 11. If Medicaid qualification is a concern, have you made certain that the documents of the estate plan provide for care of both parents, and then makes the surviving spouse eligible for Medicaid after the first one dies?

____ 12. Have you considered consulting with a specialist in eldercare law regarding Medicaid eligibility or other legal issues? *(National Academy of Elder Law Attorneys* – www.naela.org*)*

____ 12a. Are you familiar with the five-year "look-back" provision of Medicaid law – applicable in all fifty states? *(If your loved one is applying for Medicaid benefits, state agencies are authorized to go back five years to review their financial records to see what gifts have been made to or from the trust. Depending on what is found, the state may be entitled to reimbursement. Please consult a qualified attorney.)*

____ 13. Is the language of any of the current or revised documents nebulous? *(If so, have you retained a trust attorney to make revisions?)*

___ 14. When one parent dies, is the trust immediately set in stone? *(If so, move swiftly to resolve problems while both parties are still alive and lucid.)*

Chapter 11:
Estate Planning
NOTES: SUMMARY OF "NO" POINTS

12

Investment Advisors

*M**y comments to you:** If, over the years, you have not been deeply and continuously involved with your parents and their investment advisor, you may be astonished at the level of financial intimacy and detail they have shared with the advisor. If your parents are elderly and have been working with the same person for many years, you may also be astonished at the level and extent of personal services the advisor may have rendered to your parents.*

As with bankers and attorneys, the time to get to know your parents' investment advisor is while your parents are still able. Please be certain you and they explain the current situation as well as the desired outcome in terms of their investment objectives. There are a number of resources financial advisors can draw upon to satisfy everyone's needs without inadvertently creating future tax liabilities for all concerned.

QUESTIONS: Investment Advisors (Yes or No)

____ 1. Do your parents have an investment advisor?

____ 1a. If so, have you met that person?

___ 1b. If you have not, have you and your parents discussed plans for you to do so?

___ 2.   Have you and your parent come to an agreement on the level of involvement to be granted to the investment advisor?

___ 3.   Have you and your parent completed all necessary compliance forms to permit the investment advisor to act on behalf of your parent?

___ 4.   Do you know the degree of computer access the advisor has to their accounts?

___ 5.   Have you provided the investment advisor with all data he or she will need to perform the advisory services you and your parent want performed?

___ 6.   Have you verified with the investment advisor that any changes made to your parent's estate planning documents or trust will not bring negative tax repercussions either to your parent or to you?

___ 7.   Have you confirmed that the investment advisor has all the information about one or both parents' pension accounts?

___ 8.   Do you know if the investment advisor needs new copies of any of the estate planning or trust documents?

___ 9.   Based on any new or modified existing estate planning or trust documents, have you updated the investment advisor's records as needed?

___ 10. Have you obtained legal advice regarding how your parent's accounts should be held: either inside or outside of the trust?

___ 11. Are you certain that each asset is properly titled?

___ 12. Is each beneficiary properly designated?

___ 13. Are all appropriate legal documents available (i.e. birth certificate, marriage license, Social Security card and – when the time comes – certified death certificates?)

___ 14. Have you considered suggesting your parent introduce the investment advisor to the CPA and the attorney with the intent of possibly authorizing the three of them to work together in a coordinated manner on your parent's behalf?

___ 15. Are you and your parent's investment advisor in agreement that, if your parent's abilities are beginning to falter, the advisor will contact you before executing any significant business transactions for your parent?

___ 15a. As an additional safeguard, have you and your parent considered establishing co-trustees on their account? *(**Please see Chapter 10** - **Attorneys** – to make certain the investment and legal documents are complimentary.)*

Chapter 12:
Investment Advisors
NOTES: SUMMARY OF "NO" POINTS

PART IV

BREATHE IN BREATHE OUT MOVE ON

13
Celebrations of Life and Burial Plans

*M*y comments to you: *Years before the need arose, Karin's Mom and Dad made arrangements for the disposition of their remains and paid for their cremations. They were members of the People's Memorial Association (www.PeoplesMemorial.org), a non-profit cooperative that has been in business since 1939. They are members of the Funeral Consumers Alliance (www.funerals.org), a national federation of non-profit funeral consumer information societies. In contrast, both of my parents told me they wanted to be cremated, but neither chose to make the arrangements beforehand. Thanks to Konrad and Marguerite's foresight and willingness to address difficult issues, that aspect of the process went more smoothly than I could have imagined. It significantly reduced emotional stress levels for Karin and her family. If this topic is difficult for you or your parents, I strongly recommend you read Dan Taylor's book* The Parent Care Conversation.

Having experienced both approaches, I know it is definitely easier if you and your parent can talk about their wishes well in advance of the need and can make arrangements as calmly and unemotionally as possible and without haste. It is like writing something down on a to-do list: once it is written down, you can stop thinking about it because your subconscious mind can relax and the thought no longer nags you.

Spiritual celebrations of life also deserve before-the-fact thought and conversation.

My father simply wanted to be cremated and sprinkled (or as Mom called it, "sprinked") in a special place. So that's what Mom and I did. Just the two of us, alone in a special woods in Maryland. A pretty solitary and quiet way to honor a man whose family nickname was "The Management," a man who loved to host parties, play the piano and be the center of things.

Shortly after Dad died, an acquaintance told me of an artisan in Eskisehir, Turkey who carved three-dimensional meerschaum statues of people, based on photographs. The more photographs one could provide, the more accurate the carving. Since I was in the process of moving, my photos were in storage, and I only had one of my parents. This is what the carver created.

Mom liked it, and so do I.

I have lost touch with my friend and do not have contact information for the carver. However, after browsing the Internet, I found a store in Turkey that says they do carvings from photos. They may be the folks my friend used, or maybe not. Their address is www.meerschaumstore.com.

What do you have that will help you to celebrate your loved ones' memories?

Both Konrad and Marguerite had lots of family and friends in Seattle. We held their wakes at home and then sprinkled their ashes in Puget Sound from the deck of a Washington State ferry. On both occasions the captain stopped the ship, made an announcement over the PA system, saluted with the ship's horn and gave us time to perform our ceremonies.

Mom wanted her ashes mingled with Dad's in the mountains of Maryland, so we held a small memorial celebration with family and close friends, remembered the two of them, and did as she had asked.

Some months before, after I viewed her body and gave permission for her cremation, I was in tears as I drove home and suddenly realized I wanted to hear loud piano music that night. I invited Karin and our daughter, Jen, to a rock-n-roll dueling pianos bar in Raleigh. Jen was the designated driver, and I, the designated drinker. True to my Scots-Irish heritage, I did my job well as I drank to Mom's memory, and Dad's too, and Konrad's and Marguerite's.

Mom loved Liberace and his music, so, well along in beers and tears, I passed the two piano players a note giving them Mom's name, telling them I had just had her cremated, requested they play any of Liberace's songs and attached a $10 bill. They read the note to the audience, kept the $10, advised the room that "We don't do death," and then blasted out the "William Tell Overture," you know – The Lone Ranger's theme song. Eight people at a table near the pianos stood and toasted "To Nancy McDonald Burrows." I cried. It was a cathartic and wonderful experience.

On a less spontaneous note, the chaplain in the home where Mom lived wanted to hold a wake in her memory. We agreed to do that and about 50 people attended, including some of the housekeepers, which I thought was nice. I brought some family heirlooms and talked about them, and some of the attendees shared stories about her as well.

Before her stroke, Mom and her buddies liked to get together in the common area on their floor and have wine and cheese be-fore dinner. Some of the other residents in this church-affiliated home took exception to public sipping, and the management caved to their pressure. Mom and her friends groused and then complied.

At the memorial, and with the chaplain's blessing, we brought Mom's favorite wine (white zin in a box) and all who wanted to, drank a toast to, and with, her spirit. Pun intended.

Please – talk with your parents about their wishes and give thought to your needs as well.

Because Karin's parents and my parents wanted to be cremated, we did not utilize the full range of services of funeral homes, beyond that of cremation. No, that is not entirely accurate.

Mom died of a stroke, alone in her unit. After she died, the staff placed her on her bed before they called us. The housekeeper who found Mom, Karin and I sat with her for some time. When we were ready, the nursing manager offered to contact a funeral home they often used. Within 30 minutes, two representatives arrived. Again, when we were ready, they invited us to step out. They prepared Mom and transported her to the funeral home. I was pretty much numb, and was grateful for their calm professionalism.

Later on, I went to the funeral home and finalized the cremation arrangements. There was no up-selling, no stereotypically creepy morticians. Only competent professionals.

I was surprised to learn that this mortuary did not do the cremations on-site, but rather at a small facility out in the woods, some 20 miles away. Mom liked woods. I liked that.

On the day of her cremation, I drove to the site, confirmed her identity, signed another paper and chose to watch the process from a little viewing room. There was really nothing to see, but

I stayed anyway. A day later, I returned to the funeral home for her ashes.

I am sure you understand this, but if you have not gone through all of this, you may not <u>know</u> it: please be prepared to become emotionally drained as you make and take phone calls to either tell people of the death of your parent or accept sympathy calls. When I went through it, merlot over ice (yes, I know) was helpful.

Neither Karin nor I are religious, nor were our parents. For that reason, I did not address the subject of religion in my initial draft. However, I am grateful to friends Diane and Larry for calling it to my attention, and to the Rev. David Poland for giving me his pragmatic and non-dogmatic input. With gratitude I acknowledge his contribution of Questions 12 – 14 for what he termed "The Nod to God."

QUESTIONS: Celebrations of Life and Burial Plans (Yes or No)

_____ 1. Are there any special situations that need to be discussed, fences mended or apologies made?

_____ 2. If your parent was in the military and that service was important to him or her, have you contacted the Veterans' Administration and remembered to display his or her military arrangement of medals and flag?

_____ 3. Do you know how your parent wants to be remembered – with a celebration, a wake, a small family service, a hot air balloon ride, just you and some Scotch, neat...?

____ 4. Have you and your parent considered what special possessions they want you and others to have after their death?

____ 5. Have you and your parent discussed organ donor programs or other options? *(Please see Chapter 9 – Attorneys)*

____ 6. Is your parent so well-known, popular or well-loved by the community that you will need to consider the funeral as an almost-public event?

____ 7. Have you and your parents made prior arrangements for cremation or burial?

____ 7a. If so, do you have the documents?

____ 7b. If not, would you and your parent be comfortable having that conversation?

____ 8. Have you and your parent discussed any special last wishes, including people to be notified, or not notified?

____ 9. Have you gathered the appropriate contact information for the people and organizations that were important to your parents during their lifetime and may now need to be advised of their death, some of whom may include: current and past employers, labor unions, the Veteran's Administration (VA) if appropriate, Social Security, pension providers, the state department of motor vehicles, insurance companies, university alumni office, sororities, fraternities, current and former neighbors, relatives and friends, business associates, merchants, civic organizations, former spouses and lovers. And certainly not to be overlooked would be possible contacts contained in your parent's computer. *(The list can get pretty long and no one wants to be left out. It is certainly worth a good deal of thought.)*

____ 10. Do you have all the information necessary to write their obituary? If not, consider this activity to get the information you need:

(Find a quiet time and place to sit with your parent and ask him or her to recount key memories. Gather birth and wedding data, important family information and key aspects of their life and accomplishments. If there is sufficient lead time and your parent is physically and emotionally willing, encourage him or her to either write or dictate to you key recollections as part of the legacy they wish to leave to you and others. Also jot down nicknames and civic awards. For reasons of security and privacy, when you write the obituary, you may not want to include the home address. If your parent served

in the military and their service was important to them, do not forget to include it.

For both of my parents, this helped them gain a measure of closure to their lives, and what they wrote gave me and my children priceless insights into their lives and – from a more practical perspective – information for their obituaries.

Ethical Wills *by Barry K. Baines, MD, is a book that you and your parent may find of interest. An ethical will is not a legal document. Rather, according to Dr. Baines, it is "...a forum in which to fill in knowledge gaps of will recipients by providing historic or ancestral information that links generations, convey feelings, thoughts, and 'truths' that are hard to say face-to-face, express regrets and apologies, open the door to forgiving and being forgiven, come to terms with my mortality." Further, "an ethical will may be: a spiritual experience that provides a sense of completion to my life, a loving undertaking that helps my loved ones 'let go' when my time comes."*

____ 11. Besides the local paper, should the obituary be sent to any professional and civic groups, clubs, associations, military publications or other special interest places or groups?

___ 12. Have you been careful not to have overridden your parent's faith with your lack of faith?

___ 13. Have you been careful that you have not imposed your faith on them?

___ 14. Can you identify the ways you are being respectful to their faith, their concerns and their values?

___ 15. If your parent lives far from you and your siblings and refuses to accept help from "strangers," have you considered contacting their minister and asking members of their church to visit regularly?

___ 16. If your parent has a life-threatening illness or terminal condition, have you investigated the local Hospice program in your parent's area? *(According to Hospice's national website, (www.hospicefoundation.org), hospice is a special concept of care designed to provide comfort and support to patients and their families when a life-limiting illness no longer responds to cure-oriented treatments.*

Be aware that hospice care neither prolongs life nor hastens death. Hospice staff and volunteers offer a specialized knowledge of medical care, including pain management. The goal of hospice care is to improve the quality of a patient's last days by offering comfort and dignity.

Hospice care is provided by a team-oriented group of specially trained professionals, volunteers and family members.

Hospice addresses all symptoms of a disease, with a special emphasis on controlling a patient's pain and discomfort.

Hospice deals with the emotional, social and spiritual impact of the disease on the patient and the patient's family and friends.

Hospice offers a variety of bereavement and counseling services to families before and after a patient's death.)

___ 17. Are you aware that Hospice can often help people care for their loved ones at home or at a Hospice facility when conditions are critical? *(There are also local social service agencies that offer home care and elderly care services. An interesting website on elder care that may be of help to you is* www.mettajourney.com. *There you can purchase a very useful book –* The Portable Caregiver – Eight Essential Guidebooks for Elder Care *by Mary Trabert and Debbie Morris.)*

Chapter 13:
Celebrations of Life and Burial Plans
NOTES: SUMMARY OF "NO" POINTS

14

Talking with Your Parents

My comments to you: Given the opportunity to go through the end-of-life process again with Mom, Dad, Marguerite, Konrad, and Grace, I would have spent a lot more time talking with each of them in detail about what was happening to them and to me.

Dad was stoic in dealing with his cancer and was reluctant to discuss things with either Mom or me. On the other hand, Mom was angry and so put out with her strokes that she could talk about little else. Both Konrad and Marguerite simply took things as they came, without much comment.

As I reflect back, I realize that I could have been more effective in talking with them and maybe helping them – and me – to sort things out and start moving toward a measure of closure.

And I regret that, since both my parents died alone, I did not get to say "thank you" and "goodbye." This is tough stuff.

QUESTIONS: Talking With Your Parents (Yes or No)

____ 1. If both of your parents are still living, have you thought about how you will talk with them about what's happening to them and between them?

____ 2. Have you thought about possible emotions they may be feeling but have not shared with you?

____ 3. Is it possible that they may be trying to spare your feelings, perhaps at their expense?

____ 3a. If that is the case, have you considered how that could be making all of you feel and how you might discuss it?

____ 4. Are there things you can say to them so they will feel more supported as they approach this point in their lives?

____ 5. Are there things you want to say to them? If so, how can you make it safe for you to speak?

____ 6. Are there things you would like to hear them say to you? If so, how can you make that happen?

____ 7. If grandchildren are involved, are there things your parents would like to say or write to them? *(I have told you that Karin is a breast cancer survivor. Early on, when death was a topic of immediate concern, I found a perfect book for her - For My Grandchild: A Grandmother's Gift of Memory by*

Paige Gilchrist and published by AARP. Had her condition not improved, she was going to fill it out for Konrad, our first grandchild. As it is, she has also helped our second grandson, Konrad's brother, Nathan, enter the world in August, 2006. She now has two books to complete at her leisure.)

____ 8.   As you listen to yourself, could it be that through your actions or words, you are making your parent feel small, guilty or a burden to you?

____ 9.   What questions have I not asked that you have already thought about and perhaps resolved?

_____

_____

_____

_____

_____

____ 10.   What questions have I not asked that you have already thought about and are choosing not to resolve? Can you explain why?

_____

_____

_____

_____

_____

Chapter 14:
Talking with Your Parents
NOTES: SUMMARY OF "NO" POINTS

15
Spending Time Together

My comments to you: *About four years before his death, Dad surprised me by remarking that he had more years behind him than he had in front of him. That was the first time I had heard that concept, and it was a compact summary of his situation. A couple of months later, he was diagnosed with prostate and bone cancer.*

Shortly thereafter, Dad showed me a yellow folder in which he had organized all relevant financial, legal and insurance documents. And later we made a day of it as he re-introduced me to his doctor, banker, insurance agent, attorney and financial planner. The tenor of these visits was much different from the first time I had met them.

"Breathe in. Breathe out. Move on."[1]

At that time, we saw each other infrequently because Mom and Dad lived in Florida and I lived in Vancouver, WA. The impact

---

[1] From Jimmy Buffett's song, "Breathe In. Breathe Out. Move On."

of his analysis of his situation brought a lot of things into focus for me. Without my suggesting it, Dad wrote and shared with me a series of vignettes he had written capturing his favorite memories and experiences from his childhood through World War II and into adulthood.

Within six months, Mom followed suit with her own recollections of their four years living in Venezuela while I was in college.

After Dad died, I typed both of their recollections and gave them to Mom as a Christmas present as a tangible record of their lives together. She liked reading the recollections, but after her stroke, reading was more than she could manage. She did not want me to read them to her, but she kept the leather notebook out and at hand.

*Karin's Aunt Myrtle is 94. She is active, healthy, very social and funny. She is also the family photo historian, having chronicled everything the family did for the last 70 years. She not only has taken good photos – she has also recorded **the who, what, where and when** in her neat script on the back of each one. Everything is organized. What a legacy.*

QUESTIONS: Spending Time Together (Yes or No)

_____ 1. Have you offered to help your parents or loved one write or tape their memoirs, or maybe organize their photos?

____ 2. Have you made a personal commitment to your-self not to interrupt or correct your parents while they are talking, so as not to cause them to lose their train of thought or inhibit them?

____ 3. If you use a tape recorder, have you made sure your parent is comfortable using such a device and that you have extra batteries?

____ 4. Are you familiar with the **Talking Books** service through the Library of Congress?

____ 4a. Did you know they provide free audiotapes and a free cassette player to people who need them? *(Mom and I spent some pleasant times together listening to some of the tapes she got through this organization. See* www.nlstalkingbooks.org *or The Library of Congress at* www.loc.gov/nls.*)*

____ 5. Have you considered setting up a specific time to read them their favorite books, or books on a topic they really like?

____ 6. Have you asked your parents what special things they would like to do with you?

____ 7. Have you told your parents what special things you would like to do with them?

____ 8. Have you given thought to how you will approach your parent in order to have the serious conversations you know you must have, and perhaps even want to have?

____ 9. Have you and your parent had open and frequent conversations about their life at the moment, giving them the opportunity to share their feelings and fears?

____ 9a. Are you doing the same?

____ 10. Have you considered how to help them address their fears and concerns?

____ 11. Have you considered that your parents may be feeling guilty or uncomfortable because they think they are being a burden to you, or that they feel they are causing you problems?

____ 12. Have you consciously sought either of your parent's input and advice on issues, so that they continue to feel valued and involved?

____ 13. Have you documented the most important aspects, contributions and achievements of your family's history?

____ 14. Have you sought their help in completing or double-checking the family tree?

____ 15. Have you planned family gatherings that will, as actively as possible, involve your parents?

___ 16. If there are grandchildren or great-grandchildren, have you made certain they spend time with your parents, with the intent of sharing and passing on family traditions and creating memories?

___ 17. Without trying to create a sense of guilt, have you pondered the thought that, while the demands your parents may make on your day-to-day routine may be a pain for you now, after they are gone, you may miss them and regret the time you may have begrudged them? *(Without wishing to put too fine a point on it, I speak from both personal experience and regret.)*

___ 17a. Have you reflected upon the dual concepts of *"Pay It Forward"* and *"What Goes Around Comes Around"* as they may relate to the time you spend now with your parent?

___ 18. Have you told them that you love them?

Chapter 15:
Spending Time Together
NOTES: SUMMARY OF "NO" POINTS

16

Saying Good-Bye

My comments to you: Dad died in the hospital, passing while Mom had gone home to get a change of clothes because she intended to spend the night. Mom suffered her final stroke in the bathroom of her unit and died alone.

Because I missed the chance to say good-bye to either of my parents, I am fortunate to have been present when both of Karin's parents died. In their final moments, I found myself thinking of my own parents. Karin and I were at his bedside when Konrad died, and Lynne was with us when Marguerite died; I used both opportunities to send a silent "good-bye" to my father as well.

The night Konrad died, I watched Karin while she slept and, before I dropped off to sleep, I wrote this poem. I am sharing it in hopes that it will encourage you to find and embrace whatever outlets you have that will enable you to express your grief and to release your emotions.

And Wished There Was More for Me

A father spends his time today
on many things.
On work, the house, the yard –
the bills, on Mom ... and me.
Lots of time on all the above
But never enough on me.

And now I'm up and grown –
And gone.
And we see each other
now and again.
He and Mom grew old together,
and I know he thought about me.

He died today and I was there.
I held his hand. I watched his face.
And I heard him breathe his last.
I felt my tears well up inside,
and thought of our time together.

And wished there was more for me.

Ballard, WA - November 15, 1995
11:05 pm
Konrad died today at 9:47 am

*Both of my parents were intensely committed to their shared belief
that it was their individual right, and theirs alone, to determine
when it was time to go. They believed that Dr. Kevorkian had it
right, supported the Hemlock Society (now called Compassion
and Choices – www.compassionandchoices.org) and made certain I knew the conditions under which they no longer wanted*

to live. *It was vitally important to them to know that I was prepared to act on their wishes. I was.*

Karin, Lynne and I thoroughly understood Marguerite's and Konrad's wishes, and when the time approached, we declined continued medical attention that may have prolonged both of their lives but would have left them with a poor quality of life, bedridden and helpless. Given the opportunity, I know I would have carried out my parents' wishes, as I did for Karin's parents.

Breast Cancer. *Karin and I came face-to-face with our own beliefs when the doctor told her she had a five-centimeter, Stage III tumor. Five centimeters is about the size of a silver dollar.*

We talked. We were, and are, in complete agreement regarding our individual end-of-life wishes. And when the time comes, we have committed ourselves to honoring the other's wishes, personal feelings notwithstanding. That brings a large measure of personal serenity. Still, the challenge will be to maintain personal integrity and keep the faith.

Elisabeth Kübler-Ross has done extensive research on death and dying. She summarized the five stages of grief with the very helpful acronym **SARAH,** *which stands for:*

- *Shock*
- *Anger*
- *Rejection*
- *Acceptance*
- *Help*

The stages of grief apply in any situation of serious loss – divorce, job termination, an unwanted relocation – anything big – not just death.

Over a 24-month period, Karin went through two rounds of chemotherapy, one round of radiation and two surgeries. I participated in breast cancer Walks in 2005 and 2006 to raise money for breast cancer research, and we relocated from North Carolina to Washington state. During this two year period, we both went through all of these emotions, many times. We learned, repeatedly, that it was helpful to be able to name the emotion we were feeling. We came to accept that they were all just emotions and will come, go, and come again.

*I hope you will find it helpful to know **SARAH** and will greet her when she is with you.*

QUESTIONS: Saying Good-Bye (Yes or No)

____ 1. Are you and your parent familiar with Hospice? (*Please see Chapter13 – **Celebrations of Life and Burial Plans**)*

____ 1a. If not, is becoming familiar with this organization a route to pursue?

____ 2. Have you and your parents discussed their final wishes?

____ 2a. Do you truly understand what they want to happen?

____ 3. Are you prepared to accept that responsibility?

____ 3a. Does your parent know that?

____ 4. Have you and your parents communicated their wishes to the appropriate medical professionals and secured their agreement?

____ 5. In accordance with his or her beliefs and wishes, have you made arrangements with the medical professionals to make certain your parent will be sufficiently medicated to avoid pain, while still honoring his or her wishes?

____ 6. Have you told your parents that you love them?

____ 7. Have you said so more than once?

____ 8. Are you mentally and emotionally prepared to give your parent or loved one permission to tell you when they are ready to go?

____ 9. Are you prepared to tell your mother, your father, or your loved one that it is OK for them to go?

____ 10. Have you told them?

____ 11. While you can never say with certainty, do you think they really "heard" you?

Chapter 16:
Saying Good-Bye
NOTES: SUMMARY OF "NO" POINTS

A FINAL THOUGHT –
GETTING ON WITH LIFE

Even though I knew better, before Karin got breast cancer, I lived in a bubble. I took her life, and mine, for granted, be-lieving that it would somehow just go on and on – sort of like when I was eight and had no clue that life would not always just "be."

Now, with greater clarity of vision and a more pragmatic view of life from a 61-year-old's vantage point, plus the increased first-hand knowledge and experience that comes with dealing with aging, dying and death, being a parent, and possibly los-ing life and love to cancer, I look back at that time and think what a blissful state of mind that was, and how precious are the people and things I love.

I have learned that how we address end-of-life planning can run the gamut from last-minute, frenzied knee-jerk reactions to denial at arms-length. I have also learned there is no right or wrong approach – only approaches that may be more effective for some and less effective for others.

So what? What can I do with that awareness?

I can make certain that Karin's and my house is in order so that our transitions are hassle-free for us and for our children.

I can make it my mission for the rest of my working life to be an end-of-life planning resource to others, to you, helping you:

- *deal straightforwardly with reluctance issues*
- *come to an up-front understanding of why it is time to face these issues, and to help you, your parents, and loved ones do the same*
- *realize that the fear you are feeling is not unique, that it can be addressed and dealt with*
- *help yourself and the people who depend on you to achieve a measure of peace and tranquility that you might not achieve otherwise.*

TIME. *Each of us has all there is. If you will take the time to plan while you still can, I believe you and those who love you and depend upon you can make the most of all the time that remains.*

If you have questions, or feel I could be of help in a consulting capacity, please accept my invitation for a free 30-minute conversation by telephone, or if you are local, in person. You can contact me at www.PlanWhileYouStillCan.com or at 800.59-PWYSC (800.597.9972).

My best to you and to your family.

Don Burrows
Marysville, WA
July, 2007

The Last Page:
Things To Do Before I Die

APPENDIX A –
SUMMARY OF ALL "NO" POINTS

The purpose of this section is to help you capture all of the questions to which you responded "NO."

Now that you have finished the book, I suggest you review each section and develop a master list of the topics and specific activities you wish to address.

Chapter Name & Page	Cross-Reference Ch. & Page	Question Number	Summary of Question	Steps You Wish to Take & Likely Completion Date

Chapter Name & Page	Cross-Reference Ch. & Page	Question Number	Summary of Question	Steps You Wish to Take & Likely Completion Date

Chapter Name & Page	Cross-Reference Ch. & Page	Question Number	Summary of Question	Steps You Wish to Take & Likely Completion Date

Chapter Name & Page	Cross-Reference Ch. & Page	Question Number	Summary of Question	Steps You Wish to Take & Likely Completion Date

Chapter Name & Page	Cross-Reference Ch. & Page	Question Number	Summary of Question	Steps You Wish to Take & Likely Completion Date

Chapter Name & Page	Cross-Reference Ch. & Page	Question Number	Summary of Question	Steps You Wish to Take & Likely Completion Date

Chapter Name & Page	Cross-Reference Ch. & Page	Question Number	Summary of Question	Steps You Wish to Take & Likely Completion Date

Chapter Name & Page	Cross-Reference Ch. & Page	Question Number	Summary of Question	Steps You Wish to Take & Likely Completion Date

APPENDIX B –
HOPEFUL RESOURCES

Google these categories and you will find a wealth of information. Here are some I liked; they were current as I completed writing the book. I believe they will provide you with useful information:

GENERAL COMPENDIUM OF INFORMATION FOR SENIORS

Matthew Lesko's *American Benefits for Seniors – (www.Lesko. com).* You have probably seen his television commercials – he's the high-energy guy with the yellow question marks on his suit. His book is a 706-page, full-service guide / directory to just about any resource a senior could possibly need.

ELDERCARE

Resources for Seniors: *www.resourcesforseniors.com*

National Council on Aging: *www.ncoa.org*

American Association of Retired Persons: *www.aarp.org*

Lifeline Systems: *www.lifelinesys.com* Provides an activation device on a necklace

Mettajourney: *www.mettajourney.com* An interesting website on elder care that may be of help to you. I know the founder, Mary Trabert, and one of her partners, Virginia Morris, from when I lived in North Carolina. Please see their excellent book, *The Portable Caregiver – Eight Essential Guidebooks for Elder Care* – available from their web site

National Alliance for Caregiving: *www.Caregiving.org*

Talking Books through the Library of Congress. *www.nlstalkingbooks.org* or The Library of Congress – *www.loc.gov/nls*

Donald M. Burrows. *www.PlanWhileYouStillCan.com* or *www.Donald-Burrows.com*

Dan Taylor. *www.ParentCareSolution.com*

EMOTIONAL SUPPORT SYSTEMS

Lance Armstrong's LiveStrong website: *www.livestrong.org*

United Way: *www.UnitedWay.org*

END-OF-LIFE

Hospice's national website: *www.hospicefoundation.org*

End-of-Life Choices (formerly the Hemlock Society): *www.CompassionAndChoices.org*

FEDERAL AGENCIES

The Federal Government's official web portal: *www.firstgov.gov*

Social Security Administration: *www.ssa.gov*

US Department of Health and Human Services: *www.hrsa.gov*

Medicare: *www.Medicare.gov*. Excellent link to compare nursing homes

Medicaid: *www.hhs.gov/medicaid*

FUNERAL, CREMATION AND BURIAL SERVICES

Dignity Memorial: *www.DignityMemorial.com*. Extensive range of services and support

People's Memorial Association: *www.PeoplesMemorial.org*. Founded in 1939, it is the Seattle affiliate of the Funeral Consumers Alliance: *www.funerals.org*, a national non-profit cooperative to reduce funeral costs

INSURANCE

MetLife Mature Market Institute: Interesting collection of data. *www.MetLife.com/maturemarket.html*

LEGAL

National Academy of Elder Law Attorneys (Specializing in eldercare law regarding Medicaid eligibility or other legal issues): *www.naela.org*

MEDICAL

POLST – Physician Orders for Life-Sustaining Treatment: *www.POLST.org*

REAL ESTATE FOR SENIORS

Seniors Real Estate Specialist:
www.SeniorsRealEstate.com

TELEPHONES

JitterBug Inc. Cell phones designed for seniors
www.JitterBug.com

TRUST AND FINANCIAL PLANNING

American College of Trusts and Estate Counsel:
www.actec.org

REMEMBERING

Meerschaum Carvers – meerschaum carvings from your
family photos *www.meerschaumstore.com*

BOOKS

Banes, Barry K. *Ethical Wills: Putting Your Values on Paper.*
2nd edition. Jackson, TN: Perseus Books Group, 2006

Gilchrist, Paige. *For My Grandchild: A Grandmother's Gift of Memory.* AARP, 2005.

Kübler-Ross, Elisabeth. *On Death and Dying.* New York: Scribner, reprinted 1997

Loverde, Joy. *The Complete Eldercare Planner.* 2nd edition. New York: Three Rivers Press, 2000. See pages 134-6 for an extensive list of organizations that provide legal information to the elderly.

Morris, Virginia and Robert Butler. *How to Care for Aging Parents.* New York: Workman Publishing Co., 2004.

Nuland, Sherwin B. *How We Die.* New York: Vintage, 1995.

Taylor, Dan. *The Parent Care Conversation. Six Strategies for Dealing With the Emotional and Financial Challenges of Aging Parents.* New York: Penguin, 2006

Trabert, Mary and Deborah Morris. *The Portable Caregiver: Eight Essential Guidebooks for Elder Care.* Chapel Hill: MettaJourney, Inc., 2004.

NOTE: Also, please check with your local public library, United Way and other local social service and eldercare agencies listed in your telephone directory.

About the Author

Over the course of more than thirty years, in the author's career as a human resources professional, he has helped others grow and succeed through his dedication to personal and skills training and development.

An only child, it fell to him to assist his parents as they aged, became infirm, and died, a responsibility he embraced with compassion and commitment. Along the way, his wife's parents and family also needed his help to maneuver through the maze of complicated decisions, forms, laws, regulations and heart-wrenching family decisions about whether to use medical devices to prolong life or to die in accordance with their wishes.

Learning of his growing experience and competency, friends began to ask for his advice and council.

Finding he had an aptitude and a gift for helping others bring order, dignity and a sense of calm to families and individuals facing death, he listened to family members who encouraged him to document what he had learned about eldercare planning and end-of-life decisions, and to be of service.

Discussing with others his plans to write this book, he immediately discovered a huge need: elderly singles and couples, adult children of elderly parents, members of the clergy, providers of eldercare services, insurance, banking, legal, investment and medical professionals all enthusiastically told him they needed a short, easy-to-understand and easy-to-apply blueprint written in layman's language for end-of-life planning.

Their reactions spurred him to commit time and energy to start and complete this book.

As the book neared completion and Don began to consider the reality of it actually being published, others with whom he spoke saw the opportunity for him to use the book to render even greater service.

They encouraged him to use the book as the blueprint to offer continuing education classes, public seminars, speaking engagements, corporate consulting, CDs and family consulting to help families navigate their way through this difficult time. Drawing upon his years of experience in conflict management, a unique focus of his burgeoning practice is to help siblings and family members come to naturally ethical agreement in creating and implementing eldercare plans with and for their parents, so as to avoid what he calls "sibling divorce."™

Don Burrows graduated from the University of Maryland with Bachelor's and Master's degrees in Latin American Studies and Latin American Literature. He is fluent in Latin

American Spanish and is a retired Lieutenant Colonel in the U.S. Army Reserves. He is married, the proud father of two, stepfather of two, and grandfather of two. He spends his free time walking in support of breast cancer research and helping himself and others achieve goals through personal growth and development, in Spanish as well as English. He and his wife, Karin, their Doberman, Ruthie, and two cats live north of Seattle, WA.

He will donate $1.00 from the sale of each book to the *Susan G. Koman Breast Cancer 3-Day For the Cure.*

The Services of Acorn Consulting Inc.

Mission: To ease the burden of those caring for an aging or dying loved one.

To the best of my ability, and using my book as my blueprint, I will provide these services:

- **One-day public workshops.** By the end of the seminar, participants will have a completed framework from which they will be able to create a detailed end-of-life plan.

- **One-to-one eldercare planning assistance.** Free-form help at your location to assist a person in resolving end-of-life issues and making final arrangements.

- **Sibling and family consultations.** For families (siblings and parents) with divergent or conflicting eldercare planning expectations, we will begin with a one-day "alignment process" to establish a naturally ethical foundation of jointly creating a workable eldercare plan. The needs identified in the "alignment process" will determine subsequent activities and time frames.

- **Speaker.** At community, industry, corporate and trade-association meetings.

- **Corporate consultant.** In-house presentations, consultations, workshops and brainstorming with employees and managers to provide support and ideas to help employees and to reduce lost productivity and time away from work due to eldercare responsibilities.

All services are also available in Latin American Spanish

Available on *www.PlanWhileYouStillCan.com*:
- Free downloads of articles and suggestions for eldercare
- Information-exchange forum
- Additional copies of *Plan While You Still Can*
- Companion CD and Workbook to accompany *Plan While You Still Can*

WHAT'S MISSING?
I'm already thinking about an expanded edition.
What topics would you like to see included in the next edition?

For a FREE no-obligation 30-minute conversation, please call or e-mail:
Acorn Consulting Inc.
PO Box 1800, Marysville, WA 98270
Office: 800.597.9972 (800.59.PWYSC)
Don@PlanWhileYouStillCan.com

To order additional copies of this book
within North America, call:
800.597.9972 (800.59.PWYSC) or Fax 360.386.8937

Outside of North America, call:
425.231.0085 or Fax 360.386.8937

To book Don Burrows to speak
at your organization, call:
800.597.9972 (800.59.PWYSC)

To see a video clip of Don Burrows,
please visit his website
www.PlanWhileYouStillCan.com
Click on "Media Gallery"

Servicios profesionales en español
Teléfonos: 800.597.9972 ó 425.231.0085

Quick Order Form

Fax: 360.386.8937 (Please fax this form or a copy of this form)

Call: **US and Canada:** 800.597.9972 (800.59.PWYSC)
International: 425.231.0085

Web: *www.PlanWhileYouStillCan.com*

Write: Acorn Consulting Inc.
PO Box 1800
Marysville, WA 98270 USA

❑ Please send me _____ copies of *Plan While You Still Can BOOK* at $14.95 each, plus shipping and handling

❑ Please send me_____copies of the *Plan While You Still Can WORKBOOK in large print and format* at $24.95 each, plus shipping and handling

❑ Please send me _____ copies of *Plan While You Still Can CD* at $19.95 each, plus shipping and handling

PLEASE PRINT:

Name: _____

Date: _____ Telephone: _____

Address: _____

City: _____ State: _____ Zip: _____ Country: _____

E-mail address: _____

Sales tax: Please add 8.5% for products shipped to an address in WA state.
Shipping: U.S.: $4.00 for first book, and $2.00 for each additional book.
International: Based on ship-to location and current rates. Please call for exact amount.

Payment Type: ❑ Check ❑ Visa ❑ MasterCard

Credit Card #: _____

3-Digit Security Code on back: _____

Name on card: _____

Exp. date: _____ /_____ Signature: _____

To book Don for speaking engagements, public or private workshops, individual, family, or corporate consulting, please call 800.597.9972 or visit his website at *www.PlanWhileYouStillCan.com*

To order additional copies of this book
within North America, call:
800.597.9972 (800.59.PWYSC) or Fax 360.386.8937

Outside of North America, call:
425.231.0085 or Fax 360.386.8937

To book Don Burrows to speak
at your organization, call:
800.597.9972 (800.59.PWYSC)

To see a video clip of Don Burrows,
please visit his website
www.PlanWhileYouStillCan.com
Click on "Media Gallery"

Servicios profesionales en español
Teléfonos: 800.597.9972 ó 425.231.0085

Quick Order Form

Fax: 360.386.8937 (Please fax this form or a copy of this form)

Call: **US and Canada:** 800.597.9972 (800.59.PWYSC)
International: 425.231.0085

Web: *www.PlanWhileYouStillCan.com*

Write: Acorn Consulting Inc.
PO Box 1800
Marysville, WA 98270 USA

❏ Please send me _____ copies of **Plan While You Still Can BOOK** at $14.95 each, plus shipping and handling

❏ Please send me _____ copies of the **Plan While You Still Can WORKBOOK** *in large print and format* at $24.95 each, plus shipping and handling

❏ Please send me _____ copies of **Plan While You Still Can CD** at $19.95 each, plus shipping and handling

PLEASE PRINT:

Name: _____

Date: _____ Telephone: _____

Address: _____

City: _____ State: _____ Zip: _____ Country: _____

E-mail address: _____

Sales tax: Please add 8.5% for products shipped to an address in WA state.
Shipping: U.S.: $4.00 for first book, and $2.00 for each additional book.
International: Based on ship-to location and current rates. Please call for exact amount.

Payment Type: ❏ Check ❏ Visa ❏ MasterCard

Credit Card #: _____

3-Digit Security Code on back: _____

Name on card: _____

Exp. date: ____ / ____ Signature: _____

To book Don for speaking engagements, public or private workshops, individual, family, or corporate consulting, please call 800.597.9972 or visit his website at *www.PlanWhileYouStillCan.com*